FAMILY RITUALS AND CELEBRATIONS

Edited by

John Roberto

Contributing Editors:

Thomas Bright and Linda Roberto

THE WORLD OF
DON BOSCO
MULTIMEDIA

NEW ROCHELLE, NY

Family Rituals and Celebrations is published as part of the Catholic Families Series—resources to promote faith growth in Families.

Materials available for parish and diocesan leaders, parents and families

Available titles:

For leaders and ministers:
Families and Young Adults
Families and Youth
Families and Young Adolescents
Growing in Faith: A Catholic Family Sourcebook
Media, Faith, and Families: A Parish Ministry Guide
Rituals for Sharing Faith: A Resource for Parish Ministers
Faith and Families: A Parish Program for Parenting in Faith Growth

For parents and families:
Families Nurturing Faith: A Parents' Guide to the Preschool Years
Families Sharing Faith: A Parents' Guide to the Grade School Years
Families Experiencing Faith: A Parents' Guide to the Young Adolescent Years
Families Exploring Faith: A Parents' Guide to the Older Adolescents Years
Families Encouraging Faith: A Parents' Guide to the Young Adult Years
Media, Faith, and Families: A Parents' Guide to Family Viewing

The Catholic Families Series is a publishing project of Don Bosco Multimedia and the Center for Youth Ministry Development

Family Rituals and Celebrations
©1992 Salesian Society, Inc. / Don Bosco Multimedia
475 North Ave., P.O. Box T, New Rochelle, NY 10802
All rights reserved

Library of Congress Cataloging-in-Publication Data
Family Rituals and Celebrations / edited by John Roberto
p. cm. — Catholic Families Series
Includes bibliographical references.
    1. Rituals and Worship. 2. Family Life.
      I. Roberto, John. II. Family Rituals and Celebrations.
ISBN 0-89944-224-2 $6.95

Design and Typography by Sally Ann Zegarelli, Long Branch, NJ 07740

Printed in the United States of America

3/92   9 8 7 6 5 4 3 2 1

ACKNOWLEDGMENTS

"Family Rites—Doin' What Comes Naturally" by Mitch Finley is reprinted with permission from *Marriage and Family Living* (October 1987).

"Creating Family Rituals" by Dolores Curran is reprinted, in a condensed form, from *Family Prayer* (1983) by Dolores Curran with permission of St. Anthony Messenger Press.

Fr. Thomas R. Lynch and the Parish of St. James, Stratford, CT contributed the following rituals:

Advent Daily Prayers
Blessing Before the Christmas Meal and Christ Candle
Blessings Before or After Opening Christmas Gifts
Feast of the Holy Family: A Family Commitment Blessing
Ash Wednesday Blessing of a Home Cross
Holy Thursday Blessing of Family Cup and Plate
Easter Christ Candle
Celebrating the Gift of the Holy Spirit: Ascension Thursday
 to Pentecost Sunday
Mother's Day: Blessing for Mothers
Father's Day: Blessing for Fathers
November: Prayers of Remembering
Celebration of a Birthday
Wedding Anniversary
Remembering the Death of a Loved One

Thomas Bright of the Center for Youth Ministry Development
contributed the following essay and rituals:

Family Ritual Planning Guide
World Day of Prayer for Peace: January 1
Martin Luther King, Jr. Day Celebration: January 15
Lenten Daily Prayers
Earth Day: April 22
World Food Day: October 16

The following rituals and blessings have been adapted from
Catholic Household Prayers and Blessings (United States Catholic
Conference). Used with permission of the publisher.

At Table During Advent
Blessing for an Advent Wreath
Blessing for a Christmas Tree
Blessing for a Christmas Creche
Blessing for a Family or Household
Blessings Before Meals
Thanksgiving After Meals

The following rituals and blessings have been adapted from
Enriching Faith through Family Celebrations (1989) by Sandra
DeGidio (Twenty-Third Publications). Used with permission
of the publisher.

The Jesse Tree
Celebration of the Seder Meal
Easter Ideas

The following rituals and blessings have been adapted from *To
Dance with God—Family Ritual and Community Celebration* (1986)
by Gertrud Mueller Nelson (Paulist Press). Used with
permission of the publisher.

Advent Ideas
The Christmas Creche

The following rituals and blessings have been adapted from *Family Prayer* (1983) by Dolores Curran (St. Anthony Messenger Press). Used with permission of the publisher.

The Advent Wreath
Ash Wednesday Celebration

The Office of Family Life, Archdiocese of Hartford, CT contributed the following rituals:

Family Christmas Table Blessing
Feast of Thanksgiving: Family Prayer Service

Reynolds R. Ekstrom and Lynn Mahoney contributed "Blended/Stepfamily Birthdays" and "Stepfamily Supper."

Gerri Ann and Ken Goeway contributed "At Home Celebration When A Child Marries."

Faith Mauro, RSM, of the Center for Youth Ministry Development contributed "Wake Service: Death in the Family."

Rosie Piña contributed "Passing on Cultural Traditions."

"The Home Altar" has been adapted from *Hispanic Devotional Piety* (1991) by C. Gilbert Romero (Orbis Books). Used with permission of the publisher.

The following rituals have been reprinted from *Joy through the World* (1985), an Allen D. Bragdon Book produced in cooperation with the U.S. Committee for UNICEF (Dodd, Mead & Company). Used with permission of the publisher.

Las Pasadas, Navidad, Día de Los Tres Reyes
The Feast of John the Baptist
Kwanzaa

Lucia Day
Wigilia

"Celebrating God's Forgiveness" is reprinted from *The Forgiving Family* (1983) by Carol Luebering (St. Anthony Messenger Press). Used with permission of the publisher.

Joan McGuinness Wagner contributed the following rituals:

Sharing Meals
Meal-Time Prayer
Meal-Time Litany
Sunrise Service
Goodbye Blessing
Morning Departure
Quiet Time

Mary Stubler contributed "Bedtime Blessings."

CONTENTS

INTRODUCTION

Rituals are essential for our family life. Family rituals give us a sense of permanence, the assurance that even the most ordinary of family activities are meaningful and significant. Many of those who study family life suggest that true meaning in daily living is only accomplished and maintained by family ritual, and that such concrete ways of acknowledging life's meaning are a prerequisite for the physical and emotional health of every family member. The family is able to develop its own sense of permanence and continuity by taking the time to fully attend to the simplest of family activities; by going beyond just "getting things done" to enjoying the sharing of doing things together; by acting with a sense of the honor conferred by the basic activities of family life, which are not chores or obligations, but opportunities to "be" together.

Ritual is born of celebration of family togetherness, through attention to and enjoyment of shared life activities which develops the family bond. Family ritual is making the effort to impart dignity and symbolism to the simple acts of eating together, going to bed, and rising in the morning. Family ritual is attempting to "share" rather than just "do" what life requires. Family ritual is not just saying grace at the dinner table; it is making the effort to help all of the family experience grace together, through the simple act of attending fully to being together for a meal. Whether it is ritualizing everyday patterns like getting up, eating together, or going to bed; or celebrating important milestones, like birthdays and graduations, the family needs to establish rituals which acknowledge life's meaning.

One of the ways that we encounter God is through the experiences and events of everyday life--in our work, in our relationships, and in our family life. We may not be accustomed to recognizing God's presence in the ordinary events of family life, but each of our family rituals has the potential of helping us discover God's presence. The rituals of everyday family life and of important milestones are opportunities to share faith in the family. It only takes a little planning and creativity to bring faith values into our daily life and special occasions. Our task as families is to identify and establish our own family rituals so that we may enrich our family relationships and discover God in our family life.

The Catholic tradition provides us with a variety of rituals which can provide a sense of permanence to the ways we share faith in the family. Rituals are one of the primary ways in which the Catholic faith is shared from one generation to another. The liturgical year provides us with numerous opportunities for family rituals, especially around Advent and Christmas, Lent and Easter. Civic celebrations, like Martin Luther King, Jr. Day and Earth Day, likewise provide us with opportunities to celebrate our faith in the family or with other families throughout the year.

Our ethnic traditions provide us with family rituals to celebrate and share the Catholic faith. Ethnic traditions provide us with a sense of permanence and identity. For some families this will mean affirming the importance of ethnic rituals which have been celebrated in the family for generations. For other families this will mean reclaiming ethnic rituals that have been lost and, perhaps, finding new ways to celebrate these rituals. Our ethnic family rituals have the power to help us discover and celebrate God's presence.

Through the rituals of family life, the rituals of the Catholic tradition, and the rituals of ethnic traditions faith can be nourished and celebrated in our families. *Family Rituals and Celebrations* is designed to help you with this all-important task by providing rituals that you can use in your families. Each family is unique, so please feel free to adapt or revise these rituals so that they work in your family. Our hope is that *Family Rituals and Celebrations* can be an important resource as you identify and establish your own pattern of family rituals.

Part One

FAMILY
AND
TRADITION

FAMILY RITES—DOIN' WHAT COMES NATURALLY

MITCH FINLEY

Human beings are creatures of symbol and myth. They make sense of their lives by telling stories. They drive away the darkness by lighting candles, saying words, and laying hands on one another.

Many families have never lost the wealth of family rituals. They draw from the wells of their own history and from their religious and cultural roots. Through the years, rituals have been carrying many families through the tragic and comical times of their lives.

But other families have no such resources. Many have lost the ethnic and religious traditions their great-grandparents had taken for granted. In our own culture, unfortunately, many hold dear the fiction that the family can gain vitality through the constant accumulation of material possessions and professional success. This mindset poses an incalculable threat to healthy ways of being family. Until parents face this challenge, there is little sense in talking about family rituals. Once the myths of rampant consumerism are abandoned, however, family-styled religious rituals begin to make sense.

Given parental commitment to a way of life based on an adult understanding of faith, the principle upon which family rituals and family prayer may be based is quite simple. In a family, faith-nourishing rituals must be rooted in the natural events and rhythms of family living.

Parents are sometimes startled to learn of the central spiritual importance of the family's main meal—the evening meal for most families. It has become culturally acceptable to sacrifice family time for outside activities. The school, for example, wants one or more of the kids during the family's dinnertime, and many parents take for granted that the school's demands are a priority. Or an employer asks for overtime. The employer does have that right. Fortunately, many families are beginning to question these demands on their time.

The simple fact of gathering all family members around the table in and of itself is holy. A lighted candle stands in the center of the table, and the family joins hands (or doesn't). Disregarding feelings of embarrassment, they lift their voices in simple song. Traditional and/or spontaneous prayers hover over the mashed potatoes and the cries of a cranky infant or child. The family meal may be the scene of chaos, but it can be easily ritualized all the same. This is good; this is sacred; this is holy.

Adolescent offspring are going to be out till various hours tonight. Before the dash in all directions—maybe right after dinner—the family together, with arms around one another, quietly prays the Our Father.

Parents are sometimes reluctant to start family rituals for fear that whatever they try will seem contrived or unnatural. Parents often discover, however, that soon the family becomes comfortable with a new ritual.

When the children are quite young, bedtime prayers, bedtime blessings, or both are indispensable. Mom or Dad places a hand on the child's head and says, "God be with you all through the night," or whatever words seem best. They can trace the sign of the cross on the child's forehead.

A father who wins no prizes for his singing voice croons to his kids at bedtime: "Swing low, sweet chariot, comin' for to carry me home..." A mother sings, "Puff, the magic dragon, lived by the sea..." Other parents are fond of an old Lime-lighters song:

"Train whistle blowin'
Makes a sleepy noise
Underneath their blankets
Go all the girls and boys..."

A poll of parents would prove the list endless, and every song on the list becomes sacred when used as a celebration to close another day of living.

Birthdays, unfortunately, have become one of our most secularized events. Actually this is a family occasion which carries tremendous echoes of the sacred. Some families resist the temptation to celebrate a child's birthday in a fast-food restaurant. Instead, they recall the unmatchable gift the birthday person is and blend prayers with birthday candles.

Some families make birthdays a week-long affair. Days before a family member's birthday, they have photo albums lying around with pictures of the birthday person to remind everyone of significant times in that person's life. Or while eating birthday cake, they watch a slide show centered on the birthday person. One family gathers outside the family member's bedroom door the morning of his or her birthday and sings "Happy Birthday" as a wake-up song. Then the family attends Mass together that morning in their parish church.

Parents can cultivate a sensitivity, a kind of built-in radar for unique events that will, if tapped, become revelations of the holy. A few years ago, our family gained a new horsey-on-wheels for the three-year-old, a new tricycle for the four-year-old, and a new bicycle for the six-year-old. They were quickly lined up for the official family blessing. We lit a hastily located candle and let each kid hold it while one parent said a quick prayer, asking God to bless the "new wheels" and keep the riders safe.

Some parents have located religious images, that also qualify as good art, to place on the kids' bedroom walls. They walk in procession to music and make the rounds of the kids' bedrooms. They light the candle, hand the icon or picture, say a prayer, sing a familiar song, and chime "Amen."

It's not too late to celebrate the beginning of a new school year. Ignoring the TV, gather pencils, papers, and books together on a table. Light a candle, say a prayer, and sing a song.

Parents hear endlessly that they are the primary religious educators of their children. This has little to do with books, memorizing the Commandments, or learning rules and regulations. Wise parents leave that to the second or third most important form of religious education, the kind that happens in a religious education program. Kids get the most effective religious formation in the family context, and most of it originates in situations that fire the young imagination, evoke wonder, some laughter, and a question or two.

The 16-year-old just received her driver's license. What parent needs to be convinced of the need for prayer at this time? Most parents keep this to themselves—but others don't. Around the dinner table, the family says a prayer for the driver and after the meal, they go out and bless the car.

Opportunities for family rituals are endless. Families ritualize forgiveness and reconciliation with soft drinks or a game of Trivial Pursuit. Family popcorn rituals serve many purposes—spiritual to their roots, because they nourish the bonds of family love.

One of the most important family rituals is the pleasures of the marriage bed. The sexual rituals of marriage sacramentalize the love upon which the family is founded. As this love goes, so goes the family. It is a central family ritual to attend to this rite, to nourish this pleasure—and every married couple knows it isn't always easy.

Making love is a private ritual, of course, which has profound effects on virtually every dimension of a family's life. Husband and wife ritualize their love and witness to God's presence in their relationship in a more public way, however, when they express affection for each other in the presence of their children.

Inevitably, there is the problem of older children who are "too cool" to participate in family rituals. Wise parents should be patient, invite but not coerce, and accept whatever level of participation or nonparticipation the youngster is comfortable with. If the older child decides to join in, it's important that there be a sense of this being "our thing" as a family, not just another peculiar parental idea. Only patience and acceptance from parents allow kids to gradually take this kind of "ownership" in a family ritual.

There is a vital relationship between family rituals and the quality of life in the local parish. Rituals are one of the most important ways to nourish the faith life of family members. Parishes constituted of families and other households where domestic rituals thrive are true communities of faith, places where people like to be. Parish ministers do well to ask themselves what they have done lately to inspire and support religious life in the home. Families need parish ministers who know where families are coming from.

Some of the most important times in a family's life are the times of "sacred play," times when they pause, even momentarily, to remember that there is more going on in the kitchen, the living room, the bedroom, and the backyard than just what meets the eye. At such times, families know that the God of the family is thick in the air.

2

CREATING FAMILY RITUALS

DOLORES CURRAN

One of my greatest pleasures in working with Christian parents comes from helping them instill a sense of ritual and celebration in a formerly sterile family religious climate. Although many approach first efforts with trepidation and sometimes apology, they soon discover that their children love it. To a child, once is a tradition. Many a parent, after implementing a nameday celebration or family meditation for the first time, will hear a child say to another, "Oh, we *always* do that in our family." The following are my nine guidelines for celebrating family rituals:

1.   Let the ritual serve the family, not the family the ritual.

One of the problems with the old Advent Wreath ritual (the only one Catholic families of the past could identify as a home ritual) was that the prayers and format were so stylized they prohibited flexibility and spontaneity. Many families who tried that ritual and found it wanting gave up on family prayer and went back to private prayer. The language was archaic and the words meaningless to young children. The order of the ritual was set down word for word and, like many other early rituals in the home, resembled more a "mini-Mass" than a real family religious celebration.

We must not become enslaved to any rituals. Repeat that to yourself several times. Various rituals are suggested in this book. If you feel the words are alien to your family or that another order or combination of prayer would be more effective, by all means change them. God gave you your family, your common sense, and your faith. Combine them in the most nourishing way possible.

If a particular ritual does not emerge around your table as perfectly as it does in print, don't worry about it. There is nothing holy or enshrined about these rituals. They are merely words. The spirit your family puts into them—even when it seems untidy—is what makes the words come to life.

Our first family Seder meal was a disaster. I took it all upon myself, used a linen tablecloth, candles, grape juice, and the works. Our children were very young. I handed Jim, my husband, the stylized prayers and we began. It bombed. The kids didn't understand the words. They spilled the grape juice and blew candle wax onto my beautiful cloth. I was dismayed and by the end of the meal felt a real failure. But everyone else thought the ritual was great. "Can we do it again next year, Mom?" they asked eagerly. That experience told me that I was trying to turn our informal family celebration into one worthy of a cathedral. Once I stopped trying to do that, our family rituals became more open, more relaxed, and more spiritual.

2.   Initiate at least one annual religious ritual in your family.

Tradition is what family is all about. Some marriages flounder on whether gifts should be opened Christmas Eve, as it was always done in the wife's family, or on Christmas morning, as it was done in the husband's family. While there are daily traditions, such as how the family seats itself around the table or how it observes Saturday morning, usually when we speak of family traditions we mean traditions which surround special days or religious holidays.

Family therapists delve deeply into the sense of tradition in the families they are trying to help. The most solid, intimate families have many traditions: they celebrate each person's birthday in a special manner; they go to the mountains or seashore every July 4th; they invite the same people to First Communions; and so on.

I try to encourage each Christian family to develop at least one religious tradition that is uniquely its own. The possibilities are endless. Just select a ritual or two from this book and begin!

3.   Rediscover and retain the ethnic religious traditions that are your legacy.

Once when I was speaking in Texas, Archbishop Patrick Flores of San Antonio heard me stress the value of religious tradition in the family. He said to me later, in his soft Spanish inflection, "As you were talking, I couldn't help but think about my people. They have such beautiful religious traditions but they feel they have to shed them in order to become truly American. Please encourage them to keep them in their families and in their homes."

Sadly, that's what has happened, not just among Hispanic peoples, but among the Italians, Basques, Irish, Polish, and Germans who came to America. There seemed to be a race to shed the old world traditions that gave a sense of identity to the people, the parish, and the family.

I think of the Italians with their beautiful St. Joseph's Day custom of setting up food altars in their homes and inviting people to come and sample and leave an offering for the poor; the Irish with the blessing of the fields and the wakes; the Polish with their Holy Saturday food baskets to be blessed for Easter; the Mexicans with the Posada at Christmas. These and hundreds of ethnic customs too good to let disappear need to reappear in the family.

Check your roots and reinstill a few of the more meaningful religious traditions in your home. Ask your elderly relatives about old customs. Visit the ethnic parishes in your area. If you have ties to several cultures, adopt what you like from each culture.

4.   Give your family rituals time, space, and planning.

Good family celebrations don't happen; they are planned. Look ahead on the calendar and schedule your Advent or Lenten activities, your Earth Day celebration, or your first day of school ritual. Too many parents adopt the "we'll-get-around-to-it-sometime" mentality when considering family prayer and ritual.

Of course we will never "get around to it." We must *get to it now* if we are to initiate a sense of spirituality in the family before our children leave home and seek it elsewhere.

Sit down together as a family and decide what rituals you would like to try this year. Perhaps you will want only three or four. Or perhaps you will be like our family which has the following: Epiphany, Ash Wednesday, weekly Lenten Stations of the Cross, family reconciliation, Seder dinner, Pentecost, namedays, wedding anniversary, Mother's Day, Father's Day, Mary ritual, back-to-school ritual, All Saints, Thanksgiving, daily Advent and various Christmas rituals.

Believe me, we never intended to have so many. But once the children got into ritual and celebration, they liked the intimate family bonding and looked forward to these times of sharing.

Few of our rituals are long, maybe 20 minutes at the most. But they require planning. Someone has to be in charge—a parent at first, but a child does nicely once he or she gets old enough and familiar enough with the season.

Some families like to celebrate in the living room, others around the family table, still others outside if the weather cooperates. Find your family's special time and place. Scheduling time to gather today's family together all at once is a remarkable feat in families where the cheerleader has to leave before the paperboy gets home, or where family life becomes a series of notes on the refrigerator.

We find the time directly after evening dinner or a Sunday afternoon the best for our family celebrations, but you might prefer bedtime, before dinner, or Saturdays. Whatever you choose, do not try to work your celebration in before an important television program. It's defeating to condense a celebration meant to relax and bind the family into 12 minutes because a TV show is on at 8:00 p.m.

5.   Get a book or two on family prayer and ritual.

If you own this book, you already have one. If not, get one for yourself and ask your parish to supply a variety of aids. You can't be expected to know prayers and rituals by heart, particularly if you don't have a history of them in your own childhood family. Every home should have a copy of *Catholic Household Prayers and Blessings*, prepared by the Catholic Bishops of the United States. Every family should have a family Bible, like the New American Bible or the New Revised Standard Version. The American Bible Society has prepared a Good News Family Bible. Bibles are available through most bookstores.

6. Share responsibility for celebration and ritual among all family members.

Ritual and celebration should not be Mom's job but everyone's privilege. If one parent, usually the mother, takes ownership of it, she finds herself in the position of having to beg, defend, and cajole other family members into participating. Distribute responsibilities early. Even the youngest child can be made responsible for drawing a picture or choosing a song. Others can take charge of prayers, centerpieces, and readings. During Advent, let each member take turns being responsible for the daily ritual. Encourage children to originate ideas for new rituals and occasions.

7. Open your family celebrations to a wider family.

When I work with families in learning to celebrate, I encourage them to open the family circle to others. The very essence of celebration is expansion—expanding beyond ourselves, beyond our own family, beyond our Christian horizons. Invite people whose families live far away, shut-ins, widows and widowers, older adults, single adults, and family friends.

8. Overcome awkwardness and embarrassment by celebrating first with those who are comfortable with it.

If you are one of those families who find it hard to pray or sing aloud together, to hold hands, or to meditate together because you have never done it that way before, then ask a celebrating family if you can join them for an Advent or Lenten ritual so you can see how it is done. Or ask a parish staff member, like a priest, director of religious education or pastoral minister, for some demonstration celebrations or group rituals. Some parishes begin by having a family Advent Wreath ceremony the afternoon of the first Sunday in Advent for all the families in the parish. Families can then take the ceremony and the spirit of it home with them to replicate during Advent.

If you have teens it is a bit harder to get celebrations started. Don't force them. Invite them to help with the music. Usually they are quite good at that. Let the younger children lead you into the prayers and sense of celebration. Their sense of embarrassment isn't yet developed and their refreshing candor and participation can make the rest of the family comfortable.

If you have a spouse who doesn't want to be involved, ask your spouse to join you but to play no active role until comfortable with it. Ask one of the children to do the readings, another to do the prayers, and so on. If your spouse refuses to have any part of a spiritual ritual at home, go ahead and have one anyway. Don't deny the rest of the family the experience simply because one parent is uptight. If the children ask why Dad or Mom isn't present, tell them you aren't really sure and suggest the child ask the absent parent.

9.   Help other families learn to celebrate God openly and lovingly.

Faith and celebration are meant to be shared. Once your family has tasted religious tradition and celebration in the home, you will want more. Avoid the temptation to nurture it for your own sake. Once you feel you have established a comfortable degree of celebration in your family, offer to serve on the parish liturgy committee and suggest ideas to help other families learn to pray and ritualize together. Work at making the Mass more participatory. Offer to become a demonstrating family for parish family workshops. Foster a parents' discussion group. In other words, take the blessings you have experienced from your family rituals and pass them on. That's the way of the Good News.

3

FAMILY RITUAL PLANNING GUIDE

THOMAS BRIGHT

Prayer is many things. Time to share concerns and hopes. Time to be thankful and reflective. Time to dance, sing, and be boisterous. Time to be apart with God. Time to celebrate God's presence in family and in community.

Praying together as a family can be a wonderful way of supporting, affirming, and celebrating who we are as God's people. But it takes time and a bit of advance planning. The lists that follow are designed to help families organize for prayer.

List One, "Celebrating Through the Day," lists ordinary events in the day to day life of families that can be celebrated in prayer. List Two, "Celebrating Rituals Through the Year," includes a variety of Church and civic seasons and holidays that offer families an opportunity to affirm their beliefs and values, and raise their voices together in prayer. The "Ethnic Traditions and Rituals" included in the third list, challenge families to reconnect with their ethnic/national roots and celebrate how God speaks to them through the rich traditions of their culture.

Look over the lists as a family. Identify ways of praying that will be meaningful for you, that will speak in the language that your family understands, and draw your family members together in love of one another and in service to the world. Put an X next to the prayer moments or events that you already celebrate as family. Mark the moments or events with an O that you would like to give a try.

Lastly, turn to the rituals in this book to assist you in developing new family rituals that you can begin to celebrate.

IDENTIFYING WAYS OF FAMILY PRAYER

I. CELEBRATING THROUGH THE DAY

_____ Prayer for waking up
_____ Blessing before meals
_____ Thanksgiving after meal
_____ Leaving for school or work
_____ Blessing in times of joy and sorrow
_____ Celebrating God's forgiveness as a family
_____ Bedtime blessings
_____ Sharing prayer as a couple-with-kids

II. CELEBRATING RITUALS THROUGH THE YEAR

_____ Advent
    _____ Daily prayer for the Advent season
    _____ Praying with an Advent wreath
    _____ Praying with the Jesse tree
    _____ Other Advent activities
_____ Christmas
    _____ Blessing the Christmas tree
    _____ Setting up a Christmas creche
    _____ Blessing for the Christmas Meal
    _____ Prayer while sharing Christmas gifts
_____ Feast of the Holy Family
_____ Praying for Peace (World Day of Peace, January 1)
_____ Celebrating Martin Luther King, Jr. Day (January 15)
_____ Lenten Season
    _____ Ash Wednesday family prayer
    _____ Blessing a home cross
    _____ Daily prayers for the Lenten season
    _____ Blessing for a family cup and plate
    _____ Holy Week Seder Meal
_____ Easter Season
    _____ Decorating and praying with an Easter Christ
    candle
_____ Celebrating Earth Day (April 22)
_____ A Family Blessing for Mother's Day
_____ A Family Blessing for Father's Day

_____ Celebrating World Food Day (October 16)
_____ November: Prayers of Remembering
    _____ Praying with All the Saints (November 1)
    _____ Praying with All Souls (November 2)
    _____ Memories of War, and Prayers of Peace on
         Veteran's Day
_____ Family Prayer on Thanksgiving Day

III. CELEBRATING ETHNIC RITUALS AND TRADITIONS

Fill in the events and traditions that flow from your eth-
nic/national tradition that you already celebrate prayerfully in
family

_____

_____

_____

Fill in the events and traditions that flow from your eth-
nic/national tradition that you do not yet, but would like, to
celebrate prayerfully in family

_____

_____

_____

Fill in the events and traditions that flow from other eth-
nic/national traditions that you already celebrate prayerfully
in your family

_____

_____

_____

Fill in the events and traditions that flow from other eth-
nic/national traditions that you do not yet, but would like, to
celebrate prayerfully in your family

_____

_____

_____

SHARING RESPONSIBILITY FOR FAMILY PRAYER

Prayer is most meaningful in families when everyone is involved in planning for the prayer event. Regardless of age, everyone can play a role in planning for, and celebrating, family prayer. Working together on *how* you will pray helps guarantee that *what* you pray about is felt by all. Some simple suggestions.

1.   Choose a prayer occasion or event together.

2.   Check this book and other prayer resources to see how others have structured rituals for the same occasion or event.

3.   Decide on the elements that will be part of your prayer:

    - spontaneous or structured prayers (e.g., opening prayer, litany, blessing, Apostles Creed, Our Father)
    - readings from Scripture, poetry, or literature
    - centerpiece and environment (e.g., banners, photos, table cloth, plants, Bible, crucifix, candle, bowl)
    - music
    - simple gestures or movement

4.   Look at the talents you share as a family.

Some people are natural researchers, ready to see what everyone else has written, while others prefer to create from scratch. Some hate to sing or read, while others love the limelight. Some jump instantly into arts and crafts, while others never will. Go with the flow of your talents and inclinations while planning. Plan your prayer to fit your family...not the other way around.

5.   Distribute tasks based on ability and willingness.

6.   Involve everyone in at least one element of preparation.

7.   When you're ready, celebrate your prayer as family.

In many families anything done together once is already a tradition. Make a tradition of family prayer and watch the difference it makes in you.

4

VIDEOS TO HELP YOU PRAY AND CELEBRATE RITUALS

Here are several videos you can use at home with the family or by yourself as a parent to prepare for family prayer or for family rituals. Check with your parish or your diocesan media center to borrow these videos. Consult *Media, Faith, and Families* for additional video suggestions for sharing faith in the family.

Advent: A Time to Hope. Kathleen Chesto uses simple family events to teach about our Catholic faith. Advent is a season of waiting. The experience of parents/family awaiting the birth of their child speaks volumes about waiting in hope for God to break through and transform our everyday lives. [20 minutes, Twenty-Third Publications]

Celebrating the Church Year for Children. A series of innovative video programs which attempt to convey the power and beauty of church seasons and events. [15 minutes each—6 segments, Paulist Press]
Titles: *Advent, Christmas, Days of Mary, Lent, Easter, Pentecost*

Helping Children (and everyone else) Pray. Adults hunger for a deeper personal prayer life and are eager to introduce children to the practice of prayer. Sister Marlene Halpin provides a solid background for catechists, parents, and other parish ministers to help themselves and others integrate prayer into their lives. [20 minutes each part—1 video, Tabor Publishing]
Titles: *Exploring Your Own Prayer Life, Praying Together, Planning New Ways to Pray Together*

Journey to Easter. Enjoy this seven-part program, one segment for each week of Lent and Easter, as a resource for the home or parish. The viewer is guided on a journey to Easter through

the use of Scripture, drama, and stories that deal with the
concerns of life and the joys of our reunions with Christ. [15
minutes each—7 segments, Oblate Media and Franciscan
Communications]

Little Visits With God. Families for generations have made the
best-selling book "More Little Visits with God" a vital part of
their sharing times. Now bring children the same faith-
building opportunities along with the excitement and impact
of video. [70 minutes each—2 videos, Don Bosco Multimedia]
Volume 1: A video of family devotions; each story is five to
    eight minutes, either animated, live, or puppet. The guide
    includes discussion questions, Scripture reading, and
    prayer for each story.
Volume 2: Ten additional stories include the power of prayer,
    forgiveness, watching your words, and more...

Loaves of Thanksgiving. Many parishioners perceive the Mass
as a routine and repetitious ceremony rather than a celebration. *Loaves of Thanksgiving* presents the five aspects of the
liturgy that call us to a greater understanding of what celebrating the Eucharist really means. Through real life minidramas,
the video reveals ways in which participating in the Eucharist
transforms peoples' lives and so begins to transform parish
life. We come to see that faith, participation, worship, community, and sacrifice are all symbolic "loaves" of thanksgiving.
[30 minutes, Franciscan Communications]

Prayer in Your Home. Modern life tends to disrupt families.
Pressures of work, social commitments, hobbies, and leisure
activities pull family members in different directions. *Prayer in
Your Home* presents the enriching possibilities of family prayer
under five symbolic home activities: sharing a meal, preparing
for sleep, sharing our stories, experiencing consolation, and
celebrating a special event. [30 minutes, Franciscan Communi-
cations]

Preparing for Christmas I and II. These are two four-part
videos hosted by Fr. Anthony Scannell which use stories,

songs, Scripture readings, dramatized stories, photography, and reflective prayer. [11–18 minute segments—2 videos, Franciscan Communications]
Part I: *Waiting, Hoping, Preparing, Giving and Receiving.*
Part II: *The Child in Us, Santa Clausing, The Perfect Gift, The Journey to Bethlehem*

The Seven Circles of Prayer. Here is an inspiring combination of photography, dramatic vignettes, and commentary...all to help the viewer meet God in prayer. The image of seven concentric circles conveys a sense of wholeness to the life of prayer. Prayer is shown to be a very personal interior experience and yet as no escape from the world. [32 minutes, Oblate Media and Franciscan Communications]

The Story Tree/Holidays. A treasure to celebrate life! Elaine Ward presents charming tales of fun and fantasy that help children appreciate the religious meaning of various holidays. [4–10 minutes each—6 segments, Tabor Publishing]
Titles: *Colors, Spinner's Christmas Gift, On Halloween, A Beautiful Valentine, The Thanksgiving Feast, An Easter Story*

The Story Tree/Manners and Caring
Children enjoy the rich reward of caring for others. These delightful stories by Elaine Ward invite youngsters to live as children of God, to care for one another as God cares for them. [5–9 minutes each—6 segments, Tabor Publishing]
Titles: *Derrik the Dragon, Lunch with Arnie, D.D. the Donkey, I'm Sorry, Grandmother Bear's Story, The Riddle of the Jungle*

Part Two

FAMILIES CELEBRATING RITUALS THROUGH THE YEAR

ADVENT SEASON

During the Advent season, both the parish community and the home church reflect on the fact that the God of love has come to visit the people. All peoples now have a companion of love who will help them love others in new and freer ways. Both the parish and home can set up an Advent wreath in their gathering space. Each week of Advent prepares us to open our heart to God so that at Christmas our communities of faith will be renewed in their relationships with each other.

AT TABLE DURING ADVENT

Advent candles may be lighted as the leader says:

Blessed are you, Lord, God of all creation:
in the darkness and in the light.
Blessed are you
in this food and in our sharing.
Blessed are you as we wait in joyful hope
for the coming of our savior, Jesus Christ.

All: For the kingdom, the power, and the glory are yours, now and for ever.

Leader: Come, Lord Jesus!

All: Come quickly!

ADVENT DAILY PRAYERS

The following prayers can be said daily at family meals as well as in the family gathering place.

FORMAT

Family members gather around the Advent wreath before the evening meal begins.

Family Leader: Let us begin our prayer of waiting for the Lord.

One family member lights the weekly candle(s).

All: Our hope is in the Lord: Jesus is the light of our family.

Leader continues with DAILY PRAYER, listed below.

After the final response from the Daily Prayer, family members offer one another a Sign of Peace.

FIRST WEEK OF ADVENT: WAITING FOR THE LORD

SUNDAY

LEADER: Let us hear the word of God: "O Lord of all creation, we are the clay and you are the potter. We are all the work of your hands." (Pause)

LET US PRAY: O Lord, thank you for the gift of life which you have given to all of us in this family. You fashioned each of us as unique individuals. Help us to prepare our hearts for Christmas by being more patient with one another. Open our eyes of faith that we might recognize You in each other.

ALL: We wait for you Lord.

MONDAY

LEADER: Let us hear the word of God: "Nations, hear the message of the Lord and make it known to the ends of the earth: Our Savior is coming." (Pause)

LET US PRAY: Lord, thank you for the promise of your Son who is our salvation. Help us to prepare our hearts for Christmas by opening our ears so that we might truly listen to each other in our family. May the words that we speak to one another become the sweet music of our unique family.

ALL: We wait for you Lord.

TUESDAY

LEADER: Let us hear the word of God: "A shoot shall sprout from the stump of Jesse and from his roots a bud shall blossom...justice shall be the band around his waist, and faithfulness a belt upon his hips...then the wolf shall be the guest of the lamb and there shall be no harm or ruin on my holy mountain." (Pause)

LET US PRAY: Lord, thank you for becoming one of us and for teaching us your way of faithfulness and justice. You can heal the hurts which divide us as a family. Help us to prepare our hearts for Christmas by seeking to forgive each other for the hurts which stunt our growth as a family. May we become both forgivers and acceptors of forgiveness.

ALL: We wait for you Lord.

WEDNESDAY

LEADER: Let us hear the word of God: "The Lord is coming and will not delay; the Lord will bring every hidden thing to light and be revealed to every nation." (Pause)

LET US PRAY: Lord, thank you for your presence in our world yesterday, today, and always. You revealed yourself to all peoples of all nations...no one can hide from your love. Help us to prepare our hearts for Christmas by accepting the love you offer in the persons of our family. Gently touch us through the Eucharist and your Word, and form us into a joyful family of hope.

ALL: We wait for you Lord.

THURSDAY

LEADER: Let us hear the word of God: Jesus said, "Anyone who hears my words and puts them into practice is like the wise person who built a house on rock." (Pause)

LET US PRAY: Lord, thank you for your words of eternal life that are our stronghold and our rock of safety. The secret of inner peace, joy, and contentment is revealed by your word. Help us to prepare our hearts for Christmas by spending time together, as a family, resting in and sharing your word.

ALL: We wait for you Lord.

FRIDAY

LEADER: Let us hear the word of God: "As Jesus moved on from Capernaum, two blind men came after him crying out, 'Son of David, have pity on us!' Jesus said, 'Are you confident that I can do this?' 'Yes, Lord,' they replied. At that he touched their eyes and said, 'Because of your faith, you shall be cured'." (Pause)

LET US PRAY: Lord, thank you for our gift of faith. We are confident that you can heal us as a family of all sorrows and disappointments. What gift can we give you in return? Help us to prepare our hearts for Christmas by making time to laugh as a family while remembering all the crazy and fun times we have shared through the years.

ALL: We wait for you Lord.

SATURDAY

LEADER: Let us hear the word of God: "Happy are all who long for the coming of God, who heals the brokenhearted and binds up their wounds." (Pause)

LET US PRAY: Lord, thank you for your gentle healing touch. How refreshing it is to know that we can trust in you always. Help us to prepare our hearts for Christmas by seeking to trust each other with our thoughts and feelings.

ALL: We wait for you Lord.

SECOND WEEK OF ADVENT: HOPE

SUNDAY

LEADER: Let us hear the word of God: "Make ready the way of the Lord, clear a straight path." (Pause)

LET US PRAY: Lord, help us to prepare for the coming of Christ by giving new life through acts of generosity to our family members.

ALL: We hope for you Lord.

MONDAY

LEADER: Let us hear the word of God: "Say to those whose hearts are frightened: 'Be strong, fear not!'" (Pause)

LET US PRAY: Lord, help us in our family not to be fearful, but to speak the truth to one another in love, even when it is difficult.

ALL: We hope for you Lord.

TUESDAY

LEADER: Let us hear the word of God: "Just so, it is no part of the plan of our loving Creator's plan that a single one of these little ones should ever come to grief." (Pause)

LET US PRAY: Lord, today help us to remember in a special way to pray and to act for the good of our youngest family member.

ALL: We hope for you Lord.

WEDNESDAY

LEADER: Let us hear the word of God: "They that hope in the Lord will renew their strength; they will soar as with eagle's wings." (Pause)

LET US PRAY: Lord, renew the strength of this family so that we may model the holy family of Mary, Joseph, and Jesus.

ALL: We hope for you Lord.

THURSDAY

LEADER: Let us hear the word of God: "I am the Lord, your God, who grasps your right hand. It is I who say to you, 'Fear not, I will help you.'" (Pause)

LET US PRAY: Lord, empower our family members to turn to you in difficult times of trouble and despair.

ALL: We hope for you Lord.

FRIDAY

LEADER: Let us hear the word of God: "I, the Lord, your God teach you what is for your good, and lead you on the way you should go." (Pause)

LET US PRAY: Lord, you are the Way, the Truth, and the Life. Teach our family to follow your example of prayer, compassion, and service.

ALL: We hope for you Lord.

SATURDAY

LEADER: Let us hear the word of God: "Give us new life, and we will call upon your name." (Pause)

LET US PRAY: Lord, renew our family so that we may call on you in prayer and reach out to others in need.

ALL: We hope for you Lord.

THIRD WEEK OF ADVENT: LOVE

SUNDAY

LEADER: Let us hear the word of God: "God who is mighty has done great things for me." (Pause)

LET US PRAY: Lord, your greatness abounds in nature and in your people. Thank you for the countless blessings you give to our family. May we who have been so loved, now love others in return.

ALL: We love you Lord.

MONDAY

LEADER: Let us hear the word of God: "Justice shall flourish, and fullness of peace forever." (Pause)

LET US PRAY: Lord, you love us beyond our dreams. The majesty and splendor of your creation is without limit. You, oh generous God, let all come forth from your hands. Holding onto nothing, may we learn this Christmas season to freely share our gifts and talents.

ALL: We love you Lord.

TUESDAY

LEADER: Let us hear the word of God: "They shall call the savior Emmanuel, a name which means God is with us." (Pause)

LET US PRAY: Lord, you loved us enough to become one of us. You are a humble God who visits your people. We invite you to come into our home this Advent season to be Lord of our home. May your peace be our peace and may we learn to share your peace and presence in our world.

ALL: We love you Lord.

WEDNESDAY

LEADER: Let us hear the word of God: "You are my rock and my fortress." (Pause)

LET US PRAY: Lord, our faith is in you and you alone. Your love for us is enough, it never fails us. If one of us wobbles and becomes unsteady, you are there. May we who have been so loved and blessed, now love and bless in return.

ALL: We love you Lord.

THURSDAY

LEADER: Let us hear the word of God: "Nothing is impossible with God." (Pause)

LET US PRAY: Lord, we don't know how to love as you love. We don't know how to forgive as you forgive. We trust that whenever we call out to you, we will be filled with your overflowing love. Our wealth is your love for us; we pray for the grace to be generous and trusting enough to give it away.

ALL: We love you Lord.

FRIDAY

LEADER: Let us hear the word of God: "The plan of the Lord stands forever; the design of Your heart, through all generations." (Pause)

LET US PRAY: Lord, your love is everlasting. It does not shift with the breeze, here today and gone tomorrow. You are our God for all time. We are your children from the beginning till the end of time. Lord, our hope is to be a family which stays together and shares with others in all seasons.

ALL: We love you Lord.

SATURDAY

LEADER: Let us hear the word of God: "God who is mighty has done great things for me." (Pause)

LET US PRAY: Lord, your love is prayer; a power which helps us to be generous. Your love is grace which helps us to forgive. Your love is truly great. Teach us your way of love, and help us to give it away to our family, our church, and to a waiting world.

ALL: We love you Lord.

FOURTH WEEK OF ADVENT: REJOICING IN THE LORD

SUNDAY

LEADER: Let us hear the word of God: "Rejoice, O highly favored daughter! The Lord is with you." (Pause)

LET US PRAY: Lord, today we rejoice and give thanks for your presence within our family. We ask you to aid us so that we may respond to one another and our church as Mary responded to the announcement of the angel.

ALL: We rejoice in your coming Lord.

MONDAY

LEADER: Let us hear the word of God: "All this is the work of the kindness of our God; God shall visit us in mercy..." (Pause)

LET US PRAY: Lord, thank you for visiting our family. Renew our faithfulness to one another and to our church community.

ALL: We rejoice in your coming Lord.

TUESDAY

LEADER: Let us hear the word of God: "Sing and rejoice... for now I am coming to live among you..." (Pause)

LET US PRAY: As we gather this day, we rejoice for we know you are with us. Help us to recognize your love in the members of our family and in those we meet today.

ALL: We rejoice in your coming Lord.

WEDNESDAY

LEADER: Let us hear the word of God: "Shout for joy, O daughter Zion! Sing joyfully, O Israel! Be glad and exult with all your heart..." (Pause)

LET US PRAY: O Lord, sometimes we get caught up in the hectic world around us, and we forget to give you praise. Help us as individuals and as a family to take time to remember how much you do for us, and give you thanks.

ALL: We rejoice in your coming Lord.

THURSDAY

LEADER: Let us hear the word of God: "Jesus rejoiced in the Holy Spirit and said: 'I offer you praise, Lord of heaven and earth, because what you have hidden from the learned and the clever you have revealed to the merest children.'" (Pause)

LET US PRAY: We thank you, O Lord, for the gift of children and for the wisdom they share with us. Let us take time this day to bless them with our love.

ALL: We rejoice in your coming Lord.

FRIDAY

LEADER: Let us hear the word of God: "Rejoice in the Lord always. Again I say rejoice! Your kindness should be known to all. The Lord is near." (Pause)

LET US PRAY: You have shown your kindness throughout this season. By our thoughts, words, and actions, may we be a blessing to others this day.

ALL: We rejoice in your coming Lord.

SATURDAY

LEADER: Let us hear the word of God: "Sing to the Lord a new song of praise in the assembly of the faithful. Let Israel be glad in its maker, let the children of Zion rejoice in their king." (Pause)

LET US PRAY: As a family, we celebrate and recognize you as the Lord of our lives. May we continue to share this message in our home and in the world.

ALL: We rejoice in your coming Lord.

THE ADVENT WREATH

The Advent wreath itself is simply a circle of greens holding four candles. Even little children will be delighted to assist or accompany parents in buying or cutting tree boughs for the wreath. The base holding the greens can be made of just about anything—wood, styrofoam, or coat hangers bent straight and then formed in a circle. Fresh greens can be sustained for the season by providing each stem with water from tiny plastic floral vials. For the longest-lasting wreath, purchase a florists' sponge wreath form (sometimes called an "oasis wreath"); the greens need only be inserted into the sponge and the wreath can then be kept well watered. Involve children in creating the Advent wreath by asking them to help secure the greens and place the candles.

The four candles may be natural-colored, or the customary three purple and one pink. If you choose natural colored candles, the colors of the season may be represented by purple and pink ribbons during Advent, changing to white/gold or another festive color for Christmas. You may have a little crib set or Infant that can be placed reverently inside the wreath by little hands, or you can change the center decoration as the season moves on.

The Advent wreath may be used as a table centerpiece, as the candelabrum for evening prayer, or as part of the household's prayer corner.

The Advent wreath service may take place Saturday evenings. Using this time can serve to orient the children toward the Sunday Advent liturgy at the parish.

Presenting selected Advent texts to the very young child can be ideally done in the Advent wreath setting. The usual format for the presentation of scriptural texts could become the structure for the Advent wreath ceremony. Due to children's age-spread in the family, judicious flexibility will guide the choice of scriptural texts; choices should probably favor the younger child(ren).

On the first day of Advent, point out the symbolism of the wreath:

- The four candles represent the 4,000 years prior to Christ's coming and, of course, the four weeks of Advent.
- The unlighted candles represent the dark ages before Christ's coming.
- The lighted candles represent Christ, the Light of the World. Each week we light one more candle and that represents the idea that the coming of Christ is closer.

- The circular form of the wreath symbolizes that God has no beginning or end.
- The green of the boughs indicates hope—just as the green of spring indicates new life.
- The word *Advent* means the coming or promise.

BLESSING FOR AN ADVENT WREATH

The Advent wreath is made of four candles and a circle of branches. Before lighting the first candle, the household gathers for this blessing.

All: In the name of the Father, and of the Son, and of the Holy Spirit. Amen.

Leader: Our help is in the name of the Lord.

All: Who made heaven and earth.

The leader may use these or similar words to introduce the blessing:

In the short days and long nights of Advent, we realize how we were always waiting for deliverance, always needing salvation by our God. Around this wreath, we shall remember God's promise.

SCRIPTURE READING

Listen to the words of the prophet Isaiah:

The people who walked in darkness have seen a great light; upon those who dwelt in the land of gloom a light has shone. You have brought them abundant joy and great rejoicing.

This is the Word of the Lord.

(The family's Bible may be used for an alternate reading, such as Isaiah 63:16–17 or Isaiah 64:2–7.)

All: Thanks be to God.

After a time of silence, all join in prayers of intercession and in the Lord's Prayer.

Leader: Let us now pray for God's blessing upon us and upon this wreath. *(Short silence)*
Lord our God, we praise you for your child, Jesus Christ: the Emmanuel, the hope of the peoples,
the wisdom that teaches and guides us, the Savior of every nation.
Lord God, let your blessing come upon us
as we light the candles of this wreath.
May the wreath and its light be a sign of Christ's promise to bring us salvation.
May he come quickly and not delay.

We ask this through Christ our Lord.

All: Amen.

Light the first candle.

Leader: Let us bless the Lord.

All: (Making the sign of the cross) Thanks be to God.

The blessing concludes with a verse from "O Come, O Come, Emmanuel" or another Advent song.

Each day in Advent, perhaps at the evening meal, light the candles: one candle the first week, two the second, and so forth.

THE JESSE TREE

The *Jesse Tree* is a small evergreen tree or just a leafless branch
on which symbols are placed which represent those people
who helped prepare the way for the Messiah, or who were part
of Christ's genealogy. The symbols start at the bottom of the
tree and progress in relative chronological order.

Children love the Christmas tree, and making a Jesse Tree
at home helps calm the impatience for a Christmas tree.
Making the symbols and trimming a Jesse Tree would be a
good family project for the second Sunday of Advent. Symbols
can be made from construction paper, felt, contact or wrapping
paper over cardboard forms, or baker's dough. Make trimming
the Jesse Tree a family ritual. Encourage each family member
to make and hang one or more of the symbols and explain its
meaning. Conclude the ritual with a prayer of blessing for the
tree and the family by one of the parents. In the weeks that
follow before Christmas, the family might spend time each day
discussing the Bible stories that correspond to the symbols on
the tree.

The symbols for the Jesse Tree are many and varied, but
the most usual are the following:

The *APPLE* symbolizes Adam and Eve to whom the
promise of the Messiah was first made. This was the
beginning of our salvation history.

The *ALTAR OF SACRIFICE* symbolizes the story of
Abraham and Isaac. God established a covenant with
Abraham and his descendants. "I will make my covenant between you and me, and will give you many
children," God told Abraham. "I will give you and your
children this land in which you live, and I will be your
God." This was God's part of the bargain, and from the
chosen people God asked only love.

The *ARK*. The Chosen People were aware of the promise of the Messiah. They were also aware of the covenant of God to Abraham. For many years they kept the covenant faithfully. But as time went on, the people forgot the covenant and returned to evil ways. To remind them of their agreement, God sent a flood that destroyed all except the just man, Noah, and his family.

The *COAT OF MANY COLORS* represents Joseph, the favorite son of Jacob, who was sold into slavery by his brothers, but who, like the Messiah, saved his brothers from death.

The people continued falling in and out of love with their God. To re-establish his covenant, God gave Moses *TABLETS* of stone on which were written specific laws of Love.

The *KEY AND THE CROWN* represent King David. The prophets foretold that the Messiah would be of the House of David. He would be the key that opened heaven for all humankind.

A *SCROLL* can represent the numerous prophets who continually reminded the people of Yahweh's covenant with them, and of the promise of the Messiah. It was through the prophets' tradition of constant correction and affirmation that a small remnant of people accepted the Messiah.

The *SHELL AND WATER* represent John the Baptist, the precursor of the Messiah and last of the Messianic prophets. John preached a baptism of repentance to help the people prepare for the Messiah.

St. Joseph, the foster father of Jesus, is represented by the *HAMMER AND SQUARE* because he was a carpenter.

Sometimes a *DONKEY* is used to represent Joseph, because he led the donkey bearing Mary to Bethlehem.

The *LILY* is a symbol for Mary, the Mother of the Messiah.

The *CHI-RHO* is placed at the top of the tree to symbolize the Messiah or the Christ, the fulfillment of the promise and the "Desired one of all." *CHI* (X) and *RHO* (P) are the first two Greek letters in the title *Christ*. (*Christ* is the Greek equivalent of the Hebrew title *Messiah*, meaning the Anointed One.)

ADVENT IDEAS

The *ADVENT CALENDAR* helps us count days. "We await a Savior, the Lord Jesus Christ." Making the calendar is a project for the family to undertake during the Thanksgiving weekend or just before the first Sunday of Advent. A sheet of cardboard cut to a house shape is the general idea. It has a window cut in it for each Sunday in Advent and a door for Christmas. Shutters close over the window and keep secret the picture or message hidden inside. With the passage of each Sunday an additional window is opened and the contents revealed. On the window's shutters one can write a prayer chosen from the text of that Sunday's readings at church. Inside will be a corresponding drawing in bright colors.

Each family member can be responsible for a certain window, pasting it in place on the back behind the shutter doors and keeping its content a surprise until the day of its opening. Hung against the window, the light shines through the picture emphasizing how darkness gives way as time passes.

A *PYRAMID OF LIGHT* is created out of four fine apples joined with six dowels or chop sticks. Three apples form a triangle for the base. A fourth apple is held aloft by joining it with the remaining three sticks to the apples at the base. A candle tucked in at the stem of each apple and fresh greens make it a fine pyramid and table centerpiece. This can be used as an alternate to the Advent wreath, when the wreath hangs elsewhere and we need something to light during the family meal. The same custom holds of lighting one additional candle for each Sunday of Advent. The apples, however, will need refreshing from time to time. This pyramid prefigures the Christmas tree.

GATHERING STRAWS to soften the waiting manger bed is a custom just right for small children. For every good deed—a sacrifice, a brave waiting, a job well done—a straw is placed in the manger as a graphic sign of growth and preparation for the Christ Child we await. On Christmas Eve, the little manger, now soft with straw, is brought in procession to the waiting stable where the figure of the Child is placed during the night. Where straw is difficult to obtain, wood shavings or similar materials can be substituted.

A *REVERSE SUGGESTION BOX* is useful when "being good" is too abstract a concept for a child. A tissue box, decorated with signs of Advent, can be filled with good suggestions. Write a letter to someone old or lonely. Brush the dog. Set the table tonight. Share a toy kindly with your little sister. Read a story to your brother. Plan an Advent meal prayer or reading for the family tonight. Take out the trash. When children have different abilities and needs, the slips can be color-coded for each child to suggest appropriate actions.

LIFE GIVING GIFTS FOR THE CHRISTMAS LIST. You might give similar gift certificates of service from your family to relatives, neighbors, friends. Sit down as a family and draw up your Christmas List. Decide some personal way you might express the spirit of Christmas, giving the gift of self out of love. Design gift certificates indicating your family's gift. Here are a few ideas:

1. Give gifts of your own creating: candles, carving, needlepoint. Libraries and bookstores are loaded with books on crafts—even making things from junk.

2. Give a plant and directions for its care.

3. Give a service: a promise of so many hours of babysitting, a room painted, a garden planted, a car washed, a music lesson, an evening learning the names of the stars.

4. Give a gift of yourself: a story you have learned to tell, a dance or a song, a wonderful recipe.

5. Give parents or brothers and sisters something of the family: maybe a memento of some event.

6. Give a gift to the earth: begin to recycle all your paper, cans, bottles, and any other products they may accept at a recycling center.

CHRISTMAS SEASON

BLESSING FOR A CHRISTMAS TREE

When the tree has been prepared, the household gathers around it. All make the sign of the cross.

Leader: Blessed be the name of the Lord.

All: Now and for ever.

The leader may use these or similar words to introduce the blessing:

Leader: This tree is a blessing to our home. It reminds us of all that is beautiful, all that is filled with the gentleness and the promise of God. It stands in our midst as a tree of light, that we might promise such beauty to one another and to our world. It stands like the tree of paradise that God made into the tree of life, the cross of Jesus.

SCRIPTURE READING

Listen to the words of the apostle Paul to Titus:

43

But when the kindness and generous love of God our savior appeared, not because of any righteous deeds we had done but because of his mercy, he saved us through the bath of rebirth and renewal by the Holy Spirit, richly poured out on us through Jesus Christ our savior, so that we might be justified by his grace and become heirs in hope of eternal life. (Titus 3:4–7)

(The family's Bible may be used for an alternate reading such as Psalm 96:11–13.)

This is the Word of the Lord.

All: Thanks be to God.

After a time of silence, all join in prayers of intercession and in the Lord's Prayer.

Leader: Let us now pray for God's blessing upon all who gather around this tree. *(Short silence)*
God of all creation, we praise you for this tree
which brings beauty and memories and the promise of life to our home.
May your blessing be upon all who gather around this tree,
all who keep the Christmas festival by its light.
May the light and cheer it gives be a sign of the joy that fills our hearts.
We wait for the coming of the Christ,
the days of everlasting justice and of peace.
You are our God, living and reigning, for ever and ever.

All: Amen.

The lights of the tree are then illuminated.

Leader: Let us bless the Lord.

All: (*Making the sign of the cross*) Thanks be to God.

The blessing concludes with a verse from "O Come, O Come, Emmanuel" or another Advent song.

THE CHRISTMAS CRECHE

THE CHRISTMAS CRECHE is something that the whole family can plan, design, or make during these days. If you are searching for a manger scene to purchase, you may find some especially good ones in museum shops during this season. An artist or folk artist will bring dignity to the figures. Better yet, you may become inspired to try your hand at making a manger scene yourself, discovering the hidden artist inside. The process and the effort are just as important, if not more important, than the product.

As a child I was delighted with the creche my mother made. She made it before she was married during a time of illness when she was bedridden. I am certain, from the stories we loved to hear about it, that her creative experience was deep and healing. I wonder how many neighborhood friends, little boys, mothers, fathers, considered making their own manger scene after one of her simple demonstrations?

It caused all of us in the family to believe in the artist inside us. We loved that creche because it was not static, never boring. The heads, hands and feet of each of the figures were carved in wood and joined together with wire to form the body. The wire was wrapped with cotton, fleshed out, covered and stitched with cotton stockings and finally dressed. Because of their wire bones, the figures could be bent to sit and kneel and stand and hold. The manger scene was always changing and could tell us each of the Gospel stories as we heard them.

Mary and Joseph appeared first on Christmas Eve, searching for a place to bring to birth the Savior. Mary wore a bright red woolen travel cape, and Joseph a rough brown cloak. The shepherds lay on a distant hill with their flock. There was an angel, a strong guide and messenger who moved among the scenes, announcing good tidings here, appearing in the dreams of kings, and later guiding the holy family out of Bethlehem. I especially loved the shepherd's wife who brought a pot of soup and attended to the new mother. One shepherd always brought his young son. They were all shy at first, these shepherds, and as they approached the stable, the son was lifted to peer in the window and report to the rest of them what he saw. Another shepherd had an apple to offer the Child; a third looked especially rustic in a real leather vest made of an old glove cuff.

The glorious kings, from three corners of the world, marched for 12 days over sideboards and book shelves, following the star. As they arrived, in procession on the eve of Epiphany, the shy shepherds drew back. But Mary in silent wisdom held her tiny Son high, as though to make manifest to the world the divinity of her Child.

You can image the stories we spun around this scene, grounded in the Gospel message and enlivened with our own imaginations. It made me certain that my children, too, would have a creche that lived and breathed and was not just a show piece.

The creche need not be carved of wood, if carving seems intimidating. Papier-mache saves us from carving, and the craft stores have all types of materials that inspire simpler solutions. Neither do we have to make all the figures at once, but can add to the gathering with time.

Nor should cost inhibit creativity. We have made manger scenes entirely out of paper: paper figures folded double and cut to shape that can then stand on their own; paper rolled and tubed and taped; cardboard cut and slotted and fitted together. We have a whole Bethlehem of rock and pebbles from the beach—shapes that spoke for themselves and needed only a little paint to bring out an identifying feature here and there, twigs and greens softening the whole into a landscape.

The Christmas creche is a worthy art form and deserves our efforts and consideration.

BLESSING FOR A CHRISTMAS CRECHE

The manger scene has a special place near the Christmas tree or in another place where family members can reflect and pray during the Christmas season. It is blessed each year on Christmas Eve or Christmas Day.

All make the sign of the cross.

Leader: Our help is in the name of the Lord.

All: Who made heaven and earth.

The leader may use these or similar words to introduce the blessing:

> We are at the beginning of the days of Christmas. All through the season we will look on these images of sheep and cattle, of shepherds, of Mary and Joseph and Jesus.
>
> Father, we gather here today to bless this creche which reminds us of how you came to us as an innocent child. As Jesus reminds us, unless we become like little children we cannot enter the kingdom of God. Awaken within us today the child in our hearts so that we may more fully enter into the Christmas Season.

SCRIPTURE READING

Listen to the words of the holy Gospel according to Luke:

> In those days a decree went out from Caesar Augustus that the whole world should be enrolled. This was the first enrollment, when Quirinius was governor of Syria. So all went to be enrolled, each to his own town. And Joseph too went up from Galilee from the town of Nazareth to Judea, to the city of David that is called Bethlehem, because he was of the house and family of David, to be enrolled with Mary, his betrothed, who was with child. While they were there, the time came for her to have her child, and she gave birth to her firstborn son. She wrapped him in swaddling clothes and laid him in a manger, because there was no room for them in the inn. (Luke 2:1–7)

This is the Gospel of the Lord.

All: Praise to you, Lord Jesus Christ.

The figures may now be placed in the manger. After a time of silence, all join in the Litany followed by the Lord's Prayer.

Litany for the Child in Each of Us:

For a greater sense of play.	Grant this Jesus.
For a greater sense of laughter.	Grant this Jesus.
For a greater sense of wonder.	Grant this Jesus.
For a greater sense of curiosity.	Grant this Jesus.
For a greater sense of spontaneity.	Grant this Jesus.

Leader: Pray now for God's blessing as we look on these figures.

> Lord, bless this creche. Allow us always to be like the Christ child who is in love with his God. May the presence of the creche in our parish and homes help us to accept the wonderful gift that you are to us, and the gift we are to each other. (*Short silence*)

> God of Mary and Joseph, of shepherds and animals,
> bless us whenever we gaze on this manger scene.
> Through all the days of Christmas may these figures tell the story of how humans, angels, and animals found the Christ in this poor place.
> Fill our home with hospitality, joy, gentleness, and thanksgiving and guide our steps in the way of peace.
> Grant this through Christ our Lord.

All: Amen.

Leader: Let us bless the Lord.

All: (*Making the sign of the cross*) Thanks be to God.

Christmas songs and carols are sung, and a Christmas story may be read in the presence of the creche to close the prayer service.

BLESSING BEFORE THE CHRISTMAS MEAL AND CHRIST CANDLE

All gather around the table before the meal begins. The Christ candle is placed in the middle of the table, unlit.

Leader: Gracious God, we gather today as a family with a past history and a future hope. Be with us as we celebrate today the birth of Jesus, the light of the world.

SCRIPTURE READING

Leader: In the beginning was the Word; the Word was in God's presence, and the Word was God. The Word was present to God in the Beginning. Through the Word all things came into being, and apart from the Word nothing came to be. Whatever came to be in the Word, found life, life for the light of all people. The light shines on in the darkness, a darkness that did not overcome it. (John 1)

At this time light a candle and place it in the center of your table.

Leader: We light this candle to remind us that Jesus is the light of the world and of our family. We who follow Him will never walk in darkness. May we as members of this family always seek to be children of the Light.

SHARING THE LIGHT

Leader: We now offer one another this lighted candle, saying, "As a member of this family, I will be with you in your moments of darkness and pain. I will be with you always."

Each member of the family takes a turn passing the candle as he or she says the verse.

Leader: Dearest God, bless each member of our family. Allow us always to walk as children of the light. Help us to be a loving and forgiving family. Bless also the food and drink which we are about to share. Help us to remember that all good gifts come from you. This we ask through Jesus Christ, our Lord.

All: Amen.

Leader: Now let us offer each other a sign of God's peace.

Family members exchange a sign of peace with each other.

FAMILY CHRISTMAS TABLE BLESSING

Family and friends gather around the Christmas table, upon which there is an unlighted candle.

Leader: Glory to God in the highest.

All: And peace to God's people on earth.

Leader: As we light our candle on this feast of light may the Spirit of God that shone on the star of Bethlehem grow even brighter in our hearts and home(s) as we live our lives together.

A child lights the candle.

1st Reader: Listen to the words of the holy Gospel according to John: And the Word became flesh and made his dwelling among us, and we saw his glory, the glory as of God's only Son, full of grace and truth. This is the Word of the Lord.

All: The Word became flesh and made His dwelling among us.

BLESSING PRAYER

The blessing may be read by one person or by a number of persons, each reading a paragraph.

Oh God of gentleness, in love you gather us at this table for our Christmas feast. We rejoice in being together to celebrate our joy in your great gift to us Jesus Christ your Son.

Lord Jesus hold us close to each other, unite us in spirit with those who are distant and with those who have died.

In the peace of this season may the hungry be filled and the homeless sheltered, and may the unremembered be united especially through your love and peace at work in us.

We remember especially those who have loved us in a special way this past year—who have been bearers of Jesus' love to us. (*Names may be said aloud or in silence*).

All: Lord bless our food, our family, our friends. Help us to share our love.

Leader: Glory to God in the highest.

All: And peace to God's people on earth.

BLESSING BEFORE OR AFTER OPENING GIFTS

All gather around the Christmas tree.

Leader: Lord, we gather today as a family with a past history and a future hope. Be with us as we share our gifts with those we love. May this sharing bring us closer to you and each other. Let us see each other as a special and unique gift and as a sign of your love to this family.

OPTION 1: REMEMBERING

Leader: Let us pause for a moment in silence to appreciate the Christmas tree and the gifts around it, and to remember a special joyful Christmas memory. If anyone wishes to share this memory, please do so. (*Pause*)

OPTION 2: APPRECIATING

Leader: We are all gifts to each other. Each person has been given unique gifts by God. Let us call to mind the special gifts that each person here brings to our family. Let us recognize each person by name and tell what gifts they bring to us as a family.

(Allow enough time so that each person is affirmed and appreciated.)

BLESSING

Leader: Gracious God, we praise and thank you for all the many gifts and blessings which you have given us. Today, we especially praise and thank you for your Word of Love to us, Jesus Christ. Be with our family today and every day, so that we may continue to be a family which always loves, forgives, and appreciates one another.

All: Amen.

3

FEAST OF THE HOLY FAMILY

A FAMILY COMMITMENT BLESSING

Leader: Father, we gather today as members of a family with a past history and a future hope. With your family, we celebrate and proclaim the sacredness of our family, even in its brokenness. We recommit ourselves to be a family which is willing to pray, love, forgive, and to share with one another and with all your people.

Each one of us can make a difference in our family this year, by undertaking the following promises. Please repeat each promise after me. *(OR—Statements may be phrased as questions, with family members responding "I do.")*

I promise through the intercession of the Holy Family, to help my family become a loving community for each member and the world in which we live. *(Repeat)*

I promise to do my best:
... to pray with and for my family. *(Repeat)*
... to share with my family through word and example. *(Repeat)*
... to celebrate and preserve the rituals and traditions of my family. *(Repeat)*
... to show love and affection through word and touch. *(Repeat)*
... to forgive and to reconcile. *(Repeat)*
... to communicate honestly and openly. *(Repeat)*
... to freely share my time and treasures. *(Repeat)*
... to do my share of the work. *(Repeat)*
... to be hospitable to all who enter into our home. *(Repeat)*
... and to always show respect for each family member. *(Repeat)*

Leader: Let us bow our heads and pray for our family. May the Holy Family strengthen our resolve to contribute to the strengthening of our family. May the Holy Family reconcile any broken relationships in our family. May the Holy Family give us the courage to be committed to help our family become a community of life and love. And may the peace of Jesus Christ be with us always.

All: Amen.

Leader: Let us now offer one another a sign of peace to symbolize the commitments we have made to being life-giving members of this family.

As a sign of commitment to one another, family members may share a festive meal, with each family member contributing something to the meal (food, decoration, music, etc.).

4

WORLD DAY OF PRAYER
FOR PEACE

JANUARY 1

Pope John Paul II has declared the first day of January as World Day of Prayer for Peace. Combine the concept of New Year's Day as a time of making resolutions for the new year with the call to pray for and live out peace in our world.

PREPARE

Ask family members to think during the day of what they can do to make life at home, at work, or at school, and in the world more peaceful, more in keeping with God's vision of how people should treat one another. Set aside time in the afternoon or early evening to share your Resolutions for Peace.

SHARE

Gather at your chosen time in a comfortable spot in the house. Have one family member read the following brief passage from John's Gospel about Jesus' appearance to his disciples after his resurrection from the dead:

> It was late that Sunday evening and the disciples were gathered together behind locked doors, because they were afraid of the Jewish authorities. Then Jesus came and stood among them. "Peace be with you," he said. After saying this, he showed them his hands and his side. The disciples were filled with joy at seeing the Lord. Jesus said to them again, "Peace be with you. As the Father sent me, so I send you." (John 20: 19–21)

Invite family members to share what they think it means to be sent out today as peacemakers by Jesus. Encourage them to share their Resolutions for Peace (at home, at work or school, in the world).

PRAYER

Bring your family sharing to a close with the Prayer of St. Francis of Assisi:

Lord, make me an instrument of your peace:
where there is hatred, let me sow love;
where there is injury, pardon;
where there is doubt, faith;
where there is despair, hope;
where there is darkness, light;
where there is sadness, joy.

O divine Master, grant that I may not so much seek
to be consoled as to console,
to be understood as to understand,
to be loved as to love.
For it is in giving that we receive,
it is in pardoning that we are pardoned,
and it is in dying that we are born to eternal life.
Amen.

CARE

As a sign of affection, and support for one another's efforts at peace making, share a greeting of peace: handshakes, hugs, kisses, or a whole-family huggle.

OPTIONS FOR EXTENDING PEACE DAY THROUGHOUT THE YEAR

- Light a specially chosen or decorated peace candle to start your sharing on World Day of Prayer for Peace. Use the candle as a focal point for family celebrations throughout the year or during your family meeting times.

- Take time during family meetings for members to share how they are progressing in their Resolutions for Peace.

- Ask family members to write out their resolutions on slips of paper. Post the resolutions where everyone can see them or incorporate them within a family Peace collage. Use the resolutions as a starting point for discussion and sharing the next time you celebrate World Day of Prayer for Peace.

MARTIN LUTHER KING, JR. DAY

JANUARY 15

(Observed nationally on the third Monday in January)

Martin Luther King, Jr.'s birthday is a special day on which people throughout the United States remember his commitment to civil rights and the continuing need to work together to erase instances of prejudice, injustice and inequality. His birthday helps us recall our responsibility as Christians to create a world where everyone's dignity is respected and where all people have what they need to live full and healthy lives.

There are many ways to make Dr. King's birthday a special celebration in your family's life as well. The following ritual offers one approach:

PREPARATION

In advance of Martin Luther King, Jr.'s birthday, learn more about his life and the civil rights movement in the United States.

CELEBRATION

● Share a brief justice reading from Scripture, for example, Isaiah 58: 1–11 or 1 John 4: 7–20.

● Take turns as a family reading aloud the following brief excerpts from King's "I Have a Dream" address, which envision a world where justice and love extend to all people:

So I say to you my friends, that even though we must face the difficulties of today and tomorrow, I still have a dream. It is a dream deeply rooted in the American dream that one day this nation will rise up and live out the true meaning of its creed—we hold these truths to be self-evident, that all men are created equal.

I have a dream that one day on the red hills of Georgia, sons of former slaves and sons of former slave-owners will be able to sit down together at the table of brotherhood.

I have a dream my four little children will one day live in a nation where they will not be judged by the color of their skin but by the content of their character. I have a dream today!

I have a dream that one day, little black boys and black girls will be able to join hands with little white boys and white girls as sisters and brothers. I have a dream today.

I have a dream that one day every valley shall be exalted, every hill and mountain shall be made low, the rough places shall be made plain, and the crooked places shall be made straight and the glory of the Lord will be revealed and all flesh shall see it together.

This is our hope. This is the faith I go back to the South with. With this faith we will be able to hew out of the mountains of despair a stone of hope.

With this faith we will be able to transform the jangling discords of our nation into a beautiful symphony of brotherhood.

With this faith we will be able to work together, to pray together, to struggle together, to go to jail together, to stand up for freedom together, knowing that we will be free one day.

This will be the day when all of God's children will be able to sing with new meaning—"my country 'tis of thee; sweet land of liberty; of thee I sing; land where my fathers died, land of the pilgrim's pride, from every mountain side, let freedom ring."

And when we allow freedom to ring, when we let it ring from every village and hamlet, from every state and city, we will be able to speed up that day when all of God's children—black and white, Jews and Gentiles, Catholics and Protestants—will be able to join hands and to sing in the words of the Old Negro spiritual, "Free at last, free at last; thank God Almighty, we are free at last."

- Share together briefly the dreams you have for your family, for the people of your country, and for all the people of the world. Talk about what you can do together as a family to make these dreams more of a reality.

- Follow your sharing with this prayer:

  Lord our God,
  see how oppression and violence are our sad inheritance,
  one generation to the next.
  We look for you where the lowly are raised up,
  where the mighty are brought down.
  We find you there in your servants,
  and we give you thanks this day
  for your preacher and witness, Martin Luther King, Jr.
  Fill us with your spirit:
  where our human community is divided by racism,
  torn by repression,
  saddened by fear and ignorance,
  may we give ourselves to your work of healing.
  Grant this through Christ our Lord.
  Amen. (*Catholic Household Blessings and Prayers*, 195)

- In closing, sing a simple protest song from the Civil Rights Movement like "We Shall Overcome."

OPTION

In place of an in-home celebration, participate as a family in a community celebration of Dr. King's birthday. Check your newspaper for details on where, when, and how different groups in your community are celebrating the holiday.

6

LENTEN SEASON

Ash Wednesday begins 40 days of preparation for celebrating the Resurrection. Lent celebrates the memory of the 40 days Jesus spent alone praying in the desert. Lent is a time for strengthening our faith, a time to reflect on who we are and where we are going. It is a time of quiet and prayer, a time of penance and meditation, a time to become aware of our strength and weakness.

Just as Jesus spent 40 days in preparation for his work of redemption, so we too prepare for our own redemption. During Lent, we enter into Jesus' redemption by choosing to look at ourselves, at how we talk and listen, how we think and act, how we live with others, how we serve others and work for justice. Lent provides many opportunities for engaging in renewing activities, such as serving to others, praying, fasting, etc. Ash Wednesday is a good day to choose what you or your family will do to prepare for the new life of the Resurrection. Review and renew these resolutions periodically during Lent.

ASH WEDNESDAY CELEBRATION

Ash Wednesday can be a special day for family ritual. Begin by creating some kind of Lenten shrine or centerpiece that stays in a prominent area of the living space of the family.

In one family, a child used a large round tray and divided it into pie-shaped sections. One was filled with cinnamon sugar to symbolize the desert into which Jesus went out to pray. Another held a small crown of thorns made of rose branches. Others held a cross, a little lamb, a towel bearing an image of Jesus' face, and a little mound of ashes. This was a convenient centerpiece because it could easily be moved from place to place for subsequent weekly Lenten rituals.

Another possibility is a shoebox tableaux of the type children make at school. It might depict the Stations of the Cross drawn around the inside (little hands can do that—adult hands can't) with the empty tomb made of clay on the base of the box. This idea is effective as well as portable.

Although the word *shrine* is not used frequently today, that is essentially what these centerpieces are. In today's language, the word *centerpiece* is preferred over *shrine*. We talk about centerpieces for our parties and other celebrations, so why not for a religious ritual? Fashioning the centerpiece can be a prayer in itself for the child and/or family. It's great fun for children to sit with parents and create something that is actually going to be used in a celebration. Parents should not simply delegate the task to children; they should be ready to help plan it and create it *if* invited.

Preparation should begin about a week in advance. Ask family members to clear the evening of Ash Wednesday for a "Beginning of Lent" celebration. Talk about the centerpiece, ask for volunteers to create one, and offer to help. If more than one child volunteers, suggest that they unite efforts or ask each to create something. If the result is two, three, or more centerpieces, display them in various places and alternate using them during the 40 days of Lent.

THE CELEBRATION

OPENING SONG. After dinner cleanup on Ash Wednesday, gather family members around the Lenten centerpiece at the dining room table and open with a Lenten song.

SCRIPTURE. Read Isaiah 58:1–11, a beautiful passage which tells us that true fasting involves us in changing our hearts *and* in changing the structures that hurt people and treat them unjustly.

FAMILY DISCUSSION. Discuss Lent, what it means and how it came to be observed. Here are some of the highlights to cover:

- Lent means "spring," and it goes back to the early Church when the new Christians-to-be were preparing to be baptized on Easter. They were called catechumens and, during the 40 days prior to Easter, they repented, studied, and sacrificed.

- When infant Baptism became common, Lent became a time of repentance and renewal for *all* Christians. It taps the rich symbolism of the Old Testament when the Jews were waiting for their Savior. Passover, which we observe on Holy Thursday, set the stage for the Mass.

- The 40 days, of course, came from Jesus' going out into the desert for 40 days before he began his public ministry.

- The custom of ashes comes from the old form of penance where the person publicly wore sack-cloth (a cheap, uncomfortable shirt) and rubbed ashes all over to show repentance for some sin.

FAMILY RESOLUTIONS. Give concrete expression to Lenten resolutions by making a "Lenten chain." Pass out strips of white paper, about one by six inches in size, two to each person. Discuss what the family can do *as a family* to renew itself (see list of suggestions below). Decide on five items for the first week and staple them into a Lenten chain. Each family member decides on a *personal* pledge of renewal and adds that to the chain, which is then draped around the centerpiece. Repeat this ritual each week, adding links to the chain so that by Good Friday the chain has grown to 40+ links. (Instead of the chain, some families make a large cross and tape pledges to it. Others fashion a Lenten calendar).

Here is a sampling of the kind of pledges for family and personal renewal that might appear on a Lenten chain:

- Examine and adjust eating patterns: e.g., giving up a certain food or drink one day a week, fasting.

- Dedicate time to service involvements during Lent: e.g., working at a soup kitchen or homeless shelter, helping people in your neighborhood like the elderly.

- Increase sacramental involvement: e.g., go to Mass as a family once during the week, participate in the Sacrament of Reconciliation through individual confession or a parish Reconciliation Service.

- Participate as a family in the Stations of the Cross in the parish.

- Find time to read the Bible together as a family for 15 minutes daily; read one spiritual book privately during Lent; meditate 15 minutes a day.

- Set aside one evening each week just for family togetherness with no TV, only family activities.

SILENT ENDING. End in silence. It is a somber but appropriate tone with which to start Lent. Give a pretzel to each person as he or she leaves. This is a Lenten symbol, originally made of water, flour, and shaped in the form of arms crossed in prayer. The Latin word *brachium*, from which *pretzel* is derived, means *"arm."* Ask each family member to put the Ash Wednesday pretzel in a prominent place in his or her own room as a reminder of Lent.

ASH WEDNESDAY BLESSING OF A HOME CROSS

Many families have a cross or crucifix which hangs on a wall in their home. On Ash Wednesday, the family can gather to bless this special Home Cross. This Home Cross will be used by the family on this day and during the days in Lent.

Leader: (*Placing the Home Cross on a table*) We bless this cross again this Ash Wednesday to remind ourselves that we, as family members, are called to die to our own wants and needs and to be of service to each other. Let our kissing of this cross give us the courage to be faithful to our Lenten Journey.

(*The Cross is now passed to each member to kiss*)

On Good Friday the cross can be placed in a position of prominence in the home as a visual reminder of Jesus' great love for the people of our world.

LENTEN DAILY PRAYERS

If anyone wants to be a follower of mine, let him renounce himself, take up his cross, and follow me (Mark 8:34).

The season of Lent is traditionally a time of purification and enlightenment. We strengthen ourselves as a people through prayer, fasting, and almsgiving, so that we are better able to give ourselves wholly (heart, mind, and soul) to our God and to the work God sets before us in the world. Incorporating special Lenten prayers into our time together as a family helps us stay mindful of our dependence on God and one another, and of our need for continued growth as a family and as a people of faith.

PREPARING FOR EASTER THROUGH PRAYER

GATHER. Invite family members to gather around the table before the evening meal begins. Place your Home Cross or Lenten centerpiece in the center of the table.

REFLECT. Ask family members to think back on their day and to recall a time when they felt God's love or were challenged to grow in how they understood or lived out their faith. Allow time for silence or for a sharing of reflections on the day.

A LENTEN PRAYER. After brief sharing (or a moment of silence), the leader offers the prayer for the day (see Selected Lenten Prayers) and all respond: "Lord, hear us and keep us in your love."

A MEAL PRAYER. The Lenten prayer closes with a simple blessing for the family meal:

> "Bless us, Lord, and the food we are about to eat. May our love for one another, and the food we share, strengthen us to share your love with others."

SELECTED LENTEN PRAYERS

The following seven prayers were written especially for the Lenten season. Use one prayer for each week of Lent, or rotate the seven prayers through the days of the week.

Response: Lord, hear us and keep us in your love.

Meal Blessing: Bless us, Lord, and the food we are about to eat. May our love for one another, and the food we share, strengthen us to share your love with others.

---

1.   JOURNEY

Blessed are you, Lord our God. You accompany us all the days of our lives. Stay with us on our journey back to the Father. Give us the strength to walk together as a family, and help all who cross our path along the way.

2.   HEALING

Blessed are you, Lord our God. You heal the pain of separation and want. Heal us of all our hurts. Help us to be for others, in our family and world, the healing presence that Jesus is for us.

3.   HOSPITALITY

Blessed are you, Lord our God. You welcome us always with open arms. May we find space in our hearts, and in our homes, for those in need of welcome and a place of rest.

4.   COMPASSION

Blessed are you, Lord our God. You feel the pain of those in need and take their suffering upon yourself. Help us to identify more with those in need, in our neighborhood and throughout our world, and to do our part to ease the burdens they bear.

5.   FAITHFULNESS

Blessed are you, Lord our God. You remain faithful to your commitments and promises. Give us the strength to remain true to each other in family, and to the vision of a Kingdom of love and justice preached by Jesus in word and deed.

6.   GENEROSITY

Blessed are you, Lord our God. You remind us that all we are and have is a gift. May we be as generous in our sharing with one another as you are in your sharing with us.

7. COURAGE

Blessed are you, Lord our God. You take on our humanity and call us to be all we can. Give us the courage we need to change our lives, to live, like Jesus, for others. Help us have the courage to really care.

HOLY THURSDAY

BLESSING OF FAMILY CUP AND PLATE

On Holy Thursday, gather the family to bless the special Family Cup and Plate. This cup and plate will be used by the family only during special family blessings. The Cup and Plate can be placed in a place of honor in the home during the year.

BLESSING OF THE FAMILY PLATE

Leader: (*Holding the Plate with a piece of bread on it*) We bless this plate again this Holy Thursday for use in our home this year for special occasions. May we share the bread from this plate with a renewed sense of family. Let our taking of the one bread from this plate remind us that we have a hope in our being together in our tomorrows. When we eat from this plate, let us commit ourselves to be with others in our times of joy, happiness, and laughter.

(*The Plate is now passed in silence to each family member. Each eats a portion from the one plate.*)

All: Blessed be God and this family forever.

BLESSING OF THE FAMILY CUP

Leader: (*Holding the Cup with wine or juice in it*) We bless this cup again this Holy Thursday for use in our home this year for special occasions. May we share this cup with a renewed sense of family. Let our drinking from this one cup remind us that we are a family with a shared history and a future hope. When we drink of this one cup today, let us commit ourselves to be with each other in our times of hurt, pain, and sorrow.

(The Cup is now passed to each member in silence. Each drinks a portion from the one cup.)

All: Blessed be God and this family forever.

CELEBRATION OF THE SEDER MEAL

Enable the family to experience the relationship between our Jewish and Christian ritual heritage by celebrating a Family Passover meal. Passover usually coincides with Holy Week which would be a good time to have a Family Passover. You may also wish to invite another family to celebrate with you.

Sometime during Lent, gather the family to hear the story of the Israelites' exile, slavery, and liberation, with an explanation of the celebration of Passover as a thanksgiving feast celebrated annually by the Jewish people in honor of their freedom. (The Passover story is found in the Book of Exodus, Chapter 12.) Both Passover for Jewish people and Easter for Christians recognize that all things come from God: light, bread, wine, freedom—all good things. The Jewish prayers are prayed in a spirit of thanksgiving and blessing, just as the Eucharistic Prayers are. The Exodus celebrates the chosen people's freedom from oppression. Each Jewish person is to become aware of this at each Passover. For the Christian, the Paschal season celebrates redemption from the effects of sin by Christ's passion and resurrection, and God's gift of grace, especially through Holy Communion. Both are rooted in history and Scripture to show God's fulfillment of God's plan of salvation.

THE PASSOVER FOODS: THE MENU

Roast Lamb—to symbolize the sacrificial lamb offered by the Israelites and eaten on the eve of their departure from Egypt.

In the Christian tradition, the Lamb of God is a symbol of Jesus Christ.

Matzos—to symbolize the unleavened bread the Jews ate when they were freed from Egypt. Available at the market.

Bitter Herbs—to symbolize the bitterness of slavery and oppression. Use horseradish or spring radishes.

Greens—as a token of gratitude to God for the products of the earth. Use parsley and watercress or endive.

Salt Water—a dip for the greens and bitter herbs.

Haroses—to symbolize the mortar which the Hebrew slaves used in their servitude. A mixture of chopped apples, chopped nuts, cinnamon, and wine (this may be prepared like a fruit salad or chopped in a blender).

Wine—to symbolize the blood marking the doorposts of the Jews so that the avenging angel would pass over them. In Christian tradition, we commemorate the blood of Christ shed in his passion. Use preferably a red wine and/or grape juice.

THE SERVICE

Leader: Today we remember that Jesus and his friends celebrated a Jewish Passover, a Seder, a solemn meal carried out according to ancient Jewish ritual. Let us pretend we are in the upper room of a house. We are celebrating the passover of God's people from slavery to freedom.

Lighting the Festival Lights

Leader (Father): We, (*name of family*), light candles to remind ourselves that Jesus, the light of the world, is coming.

Leader (Mother): (*Lights the candles*) Blessed are you, God, Creator of the Universe, who has commanded us to light the festival lights. Blessed are you, God, for you have made us alive and keep us alive through all seasons. During this spring season may our home be filled with peace and joy.

Leader: Food is always blessed before it is eaten. A long time ago, the Jews blessed their bread and wine at their Jewish Passover. Just as they did, we bless ours tonight (today).

All: Thank you, God, for choosing us to be your people. We celebrate all you have given us.

THE ELIJAH CUP

Leader: (*Opens the front door*) There is an extra cup on this table. We would give this cup of honor to any stranger who should come and ask to keep the Passover with us. We call this cup the Elijah Cup because Elijah is known to have helped the poor. We have opened the door to welcome anyone who may stand outside. We pray for the hungry and the poor and wish they could celebrate this Passover meal with us.

Leader: (*Pouring and drinking the wine*) Four times during the Seder meal, wine is passed. We will pass the wine only twice. Usually the wine is poured from one bowl to show oneness.

(*The leader pours wine or grape juice into each person's cup.*)

At the Last Supper, Christ poured wine for his friends and said, "Take this and drink it. I tell you that I will not drink of the fruit of the vine again until I drink it with you in my Father's Kingdom."

All: Blessed are you, God, for making this fruit of the vine.

(*The participants drink their wine.*)

WASHING OF HANDS

Leader: We must clean not only our hands but also our hearts and minds. The presider washes his hands just as Christ washed the feet of his friends at the Last Supper. This gesture shows how much he loves us; it calls us to serve others.

(The leader washes his or her hands and then washes the hands of all the participants as a sign of willingness to serve.)

All: Thank you, God, Creator of the Universe, for showing us how to serve others.

EATING OF GREENS

Leader: We eat these greens as a symbol that nature comes to life in spring-time. Following the Jewish custom, we dip the greens in salt and pray:

All: Blessed are you, God, Creator of the Universe, creator of the fruit of the earth.

(Participants dip the greens in salt and eat them.)

EASTER SEASON

EASTER IDEAS

EASTER EGGS

In ancient times Easter eggs were a symbol of spring and fertility. An egg seems dead and yet contains new life; so does the earth at the end of winter. This is the reason why people in pre-Christian ages presented each other with eggs at the beginning of spring, which in those days also was the beginning of the new year.

In medieval times the eating of eggs was prohibited during Lent, so the faithful transferred the custom of giving eggs to Easter Sunday. Instead of representing fertility, the Easter egg became a symbol of the rock tomb out of which Christ gloriously emerged to the new life of his resurrection. The Church even has a ritual blessing for eggs.

BLESSING THE EASTER EGGS

The whole household can gather to bless the eggs that have been decorated for Easter.

All extend their hands over the eggs as one member of the household prays the blessing: We praise you, O God, for these signs of life, our Easter eggs. We thank you for the bright, bursting forth of Christ our Lord. Amen. Alleluia!

In the same way, the household can bless the Easter pastries: We praise you, O God, for sweetness and delight. We thank you for the journey of Lent. We rejoice in the resurrection of Christ and this Eastertime. Amen. Alleluia!

EASTER WATER

In the liturgy of Holy Saturday night, the presider solemnly blesses the Easter water, which will be used during the service for baptisms. Families can take home a small container of this holy water to be used during the Easter season and the year for family blessings on persons, house and rooms, and on Easter symbols such as eggs, pastry, baskets, meals. Each sprinkling signifies that all of our life is being baptized or being made holy by the presence of Christ to us.

During the year, parents can sign their children with a blessing using the holy water before tucking them into bed.

FAMILY PASCHAL CANDLE

Burn a large white candle in your home at Eastertime, just as the Easter candle lights the sanctuary at church during Eastertime. Decorate it with the traditional symbols that are on the Paschal Candle, or any Christian or springtime symbols the family would like to have on their candle (nail polish or acrylic paints work best for this).

The Paschal Candle is inscribed with an *alpha* (the first letter of the Greek alphabet) and an *omega* (the last letter) with a cross in between. The four quarters of the cross are identified with the numerals of the current year.

Put your candle in a prominent place and you will have your very own Paschal Candle to remind you that Christ is our light.

BLESSING THE FAMILY PASCHAL CANDLE

After the candle is decorated and put in place, the head of the household can pray a blessing on the candle while all family members extend their hands over the candle:

Loving God, we ask your blessing on this symbol of Christ our Light. May it be a constant reminder to all of us that we, too, are to bring the Light of Christ to others by our lives of justice and kindness. Amen.

In Greece it is a custom after the Easter Vigil to carry the "light" from the Paschal Candle home to light the lamps in each home. All our light comes from the one light—Christ. Your family may wish to carry a light from the Paschal Candle home to light your family Paschal Candle for the first time. (A glass enclosed votive candle works well for this "transport.")

EASTER CHRIST CANDLE

During the seven weeks of Easter, the Paschal Candle will be lit in church to remind the community that the Risen Lord is in their midst. The family may also light the Christ candle (used during the Christmas season) as a reminder of this mystery. The family lights the candle whenever members gather for meals as a reminder that we come to know Jesus in the breaking of the bread. (Luke 24: 13–35)

Place the Christ candle in the center of the table. As a family member lights the candle, all members of the family say:

Dying you destroyed our death.
Rising you restored our life.
Lord Jesus, come to this home so that we may continue to grow in our love for each other.

Using the Easter water, family members bless each other on the forehead with the sign of the cross. This water is a sign of our baptismal covenant with God and each other. Through the waters of baptism, we are reminded that we have been given God's Spirit and through the Spirit have the power to love as the Lord has loved us.

For the next seven weeks, invite family members to select a phrase from Scripture that will be said each day. Each week a new phrase will be selected and used for the week. Say this phrase together around the candle, and at any time during the day. The following phrases are suggestions.

> Peace be with you. (John 20: 19)
> Know that I am with you always. (Matthew 28: 20)
> As the Father has sent me, so I send you. (John 20: 21)
> Do not persist in your unbelief but believe. (John 20: 27)
> Follow me. (John 21: 19)
> ...what I have I give to you. (Acts 3: 6)
> We are of one heart and one mind. (Acts 4: 32)

CELEBRATING THE GIFT OF THE HOLY SPIRIT: ASCENSION THURSDAY TO PENTECOST SUNDAY

This celebration of the gift of the Holy Spirit is prayed on nine consecutive days from the Ascension until Pentecost. It may be said alone or as a family.

Leader: Lord, send out your Spirit and renew our family and our world.

> The Spirit of the Lord is upon me. He has anointed me to bring good news to the poor, to proclaim liberty to captives and to give new sight to the blind, to free the oppressed and to announce the Lord's year of mercy. (Luke 4: 18–19)

All: Come, Holy Spirit, fill the hearts of each one of us with the fire of your love.

Leader, or various family members, ask for the seven gifts of the Holy Spirit:

Holy Spirit, grant us your gift of wisdom so that we may know that all life comes from you and, therefore, is sacred.

Holy Spirit, grant us your gift of understanding so that we may see and accept ourselves as we are.

Holy Spirit, grant us your gift of counsel so that we may seek out help from others especially when we are in need.

Holy Spirit, grant us your gift of fortitude so that we may have the courage to do what is right and just.

Holy Spirit, grant us your gift of knowledge so that we may have a burning desire to seek the truth about ourselves.

Holy Spirit, grant us your gift of piety so that our relationship with you will be awakened.

Holy Spirit, grant us your gift of fear of the Lord so that someday we will stand before you in judgment for what we have done in response to the poor and hurting.

Leader: Let us pray silently for ourselves, for those close to us, and for any person who is in special need of the Spirit's protection and guidance. (*Petitions may be private, or may be shared aloud.*)

Leader: God, we are children led by the Spirit and so we cry out "Abba." Thank you for sending forth your Spirit to be with us at all times, for calling us your sons and daughters. Thank you for leading us out of the slavery of our own fears, and for loving and healing us. May we always give witness to the power of your Spirit in our lives and may we never separate ourselves from you.

All: Amen.

8

EARTH DAY

APRIL 22

The first Earth Day was celebrated on April 22, 1970. In 1990, in recognition of the 20th anniversary of Earth Day, President George Bush signed into law a joint Congressional resolution proclaiming the 1990s as the decade of the environment.

Environmental issues offer an easy way for families to get involved in a pressing justice issue—protecting the earth's environment for the sake of all created beings, and seeing that the world's resources are used for the benefit of all. Bringing the celebration of Earth Day into the home stresses the importance of environmental issues and the responsibility we share as Christians to treat the world with care and to share its resources with people of other countries and other generations.

Celebrate Earth Day at home by trying one of the following ideas.

CREATE AN ENVIRONMENT FOR SHARING
On the table in your dining area place a candle and a basket or bowl filled with fruit. If possible, select different kinds of fruit, fruits of different shape, color, taste, and origin.

SHARE IN FOOD AND CONVERSATION
Pass the bowl of fruit around, asking everyone to take and enjoy one of the many "fruits of the earth." As you eat, talk about other "fruits of the earth"—things necessary for life that you receive from the earth. Discuss your concerns for the world, sharing not just what makes you fear for the future of the earth, but also what makes you hopeful about the future.

SHARE IN SCRIPTURE
Use Psalm 148 or Psalm 65: 6–13, wonderful hymns of praise to God. The verses to the psalm can be read by different members of the family or members can alternate verses, asking

the parents (or women) to read the odd verses and the
children (or men) to read the even.

CLOSE WITH A SIMPLE PRAYER

Drawing upon the thoughts shared in conversation, compose
a closing prayer of your own, or use one of the following:

> Mother, Father, Loving God
> Remind us daily of the sanctity of all life.
>
> Touch our hearts with the glorious oneness of all creation,
> As we strive to respect all the living beings on this planet.
>
> Penetrate our souls with the beauty of this earth,
> As we attune ourselves to the rhythm and flow of the
> seasons.
>
> Awaken our minds with the knowledge to achieve a
> world in perfect harmony
> And grant us the wisdom to realize that we can have
> heaven on earth. (Jo Poore)

> Great Spirit, give us hearts to understand;
> Never to take from creation's beauty more than we give;
> Never to destroy wantonly for the furtherance of greed;
> Never to deny to give our hands for the building of earth's
> beauty;
> Never to take from her what we cannot use.
>
> Give us hearts to understand that to destroy earth's music
> is to create confusion;
> That to wreck her appearance is to blind us to beauty;
> That to callously pollute her fragrance is to make a house
> of stench;
> That as we care for her she will care for us.
> Amen.
> (U.N. Environmental Sabbath Program)

TAKE ACTION

You can extend your commitment to caring for the earth by taking action steps as a family, for example, participating together in the community cleanup of a local park or stream, or doing an ecology tour of your home, looking for ways to recycle or reuse resources, and to reduce waste and consumption. Two readily available resources offer a wealth of ideas for family involvement. They are:

50 Simple Things You Can Do to Save the Earth by the Earth Works Group (Berkeley, CA: The Earth Works Press, 1989, $4.95) and

How to Make the World a Better Place—A Guide to Doing Good by Jeffrey Hollender (New York: William Morrow and Co., 1990, $9.95)

SPECIAL DESSERT

If your children are young and a less formal approach to celebrating Earth Day would work better for you, try this easy idea: celebrate Earth Day with a special dessert. Make (or buy) large sugar cookies. Invite family members to decorate the cookies with tubes of colored frosting. Cookies can be decorated to represent the Earth or a gift that we receive from the earth. When the decorating is done (and the mess cleaned up) have each family member offer a simple prayer, like "Today I thank God for earth's gift of..." When the praying is finished, start eating!

(The two prayers are taken from *Earth Prayers: From Around the World—365 Prayers, Poems, and Invocations for Honoring the Earth* by Elizabeth Roberts and Elias Amidon, San Francisco: HarperCollins Publishers, 1991: 179, 181.)

9

MOTHER'S DAY

BLESSING FOR MOTHERS

This blessing provides an opportunity to give thanks, affirmation, and your blessing to your mother. Since time always passes so quickly, accept this invitation to bless your mother this year.

THANKSGIVING

A son or daughter leads the family in the following:

Leader: Dearest mother, for saying yes to my life and for offering me the chance to live and grow.
Children: I say, thank you.

Leader: For the times when I just needed someone to talk to, and you were there.
Children: I say, thank you.

Leader: For the times when no one believed in me, and you stood firmly by me.
Children: I say, thank you.

Leader: For the times when you did so much for me, and expected so little or nothing in return.
Children: I say, thank you.

Leader: For the times when I messed up, and you graciously embraced and forgave me.
Children: I say, thank you.

Leader: For the times when I was sick, and you gave me your special, loving, and motherly care.
Children: I say, thank you.

AFFIRMATION

Take a moment to tell your mother about one of her qualities which you admire.

A son or daughter says, on behalf of all the children:

> I believe in you, Mom. You are someone who is very important to me, not because of the things you do, but rather for the person you are. I honor you and love you. I love you for who you are, and not for who I pretend or hope you to be. If you have hurt me in any way, I forgive you. I know in my heart that you are God's gift to me.

BLESSING

Leader (*son or daughter*): Lord God, bless our mother this day with all good things: health, joy, love, and laughter. Keep her in your care and protect her from all which is harmful. And grant her peace and justice all her days.

All: Amen.

Offer your mother your blessing by signing her with the sign of the cross on her forehead. You may also ask her to bless you in the same way.

FATHER'S DAY

BLESSING FOR FATHERS

This blessing will provide an opportunity to give thanks, affirmation, and your blessing to your father. Since time always passes so quickly, accept this invitation to bless your father this year.

A son or daughter leads the family in the following:

> Lord, we have relied on our father for so many things throughout the years, and we often forget that he is not invincible, but rather a person who has strengths and weaknesses just like us. Help us Lord, to always give our father the chance to be simply who he is, a blessing to us. Lord, this Father's Day may we learn to love and appreciate our father, and to bless him with the innocence we once shared with him as children.

INTERCESSIONS

Leader: Lord, may our dad experience your love for him in new and deeper ways this Father's Day. May he always be aware of how deeply his children love him.
Children: Hear us God, our Father.

Leader: May we always have memories of shared love with our dad.
Children: Hear us God, our Father.

Leader: May we always have the courage to tell our father how much we love him.
Children: Hear us God, our Father.

Leader: Free our father from any injury or hurt we may have caused, so that we may be as united in love as we are intended to be.
Children: Hear us God, our Father.

Leader: May we always walk proudly with our father in times of prosperity and in times of need, and humbly support him as he has supported us.
Children: Hear us God, our Father.

Leader: May we have the courage to forgive our father any hurts we have experienced and accept him in his brokenness.
Children: Hear us God, our Father.

AFFIRMATION

Take a moment to tell your father about one of his qualities which you admire.

On behalf of all the children, one son or daughter says:

I believe in you, Dad. You are someone who is very important to me, not because of the things you do, but rather for the person you are. I honor you and love you. I love you for who you are, and not for who I pretend or hope you to be. If you have hurt me in any way, I forgive you. I know in my heart that you are God's gift to me.

BLESSING

Leader: Lord God, bless our father this day with all good things: health, joy, love, and laughter. Keep him in your care and protect him from all which is harmful. And grant him peace and justice all his days.

All: Amen.

Offer your father your blessing by signing him with the sign of the cross on his forehead. You may also ask your father to bless you in the same way.

WORLD FOOD DAY

OCTOBER 16

World Food Day was created by the world's representatives to the United Nations. It is celebrated every year on October 16th in over 100 countries around the world. The purpose of World Food Day is to focus people's attention on food and to get all the world's people working together to find solutions to problems like food distribution and hunger.

World Food Day provides an opportunity for families to learn more about where our food comes from and why some people in our world go hungry. It also offers a wonderful chance to thank God for the variety of foods that we have, and to commit ourselves as families to helping other people get the food they need to survive.

World Food Day can be a good time to celebrate, in family groupings, our connectedness with people around the earth. It is also a good time to help children understand the connection between faith and helping others in need. It is important that children and families be involved in service of others; it is equally important that they understand why they are involved, that faith calls them to work together with Jesus to help people in need around the neighborhood and around the world.

Learning, praying, and serving are all part of the Christian message. World Food Day is a wonderful time to bring these three dimensions of faith together as a family. Bring the importance of World Food Day into your home in any of the following ways:

Setting the Table at Meal Time: Purchase or create placemats that feature a picture of the world and/or its people. Cut placemats from old maps from different parts of the country or world. Put a small globe in the middle of your table or off to the side where it can be seen by all. Decorate the table with drawings, pictures, or objects from different countries.

Deciding on a Menu: Vote on the family's favorite meal and serve it with fanfare! Work together at preparing an ethnic meal that ties your family in with people from another part of the world. Invite family or friends for a pot-luck supper or smorgasbord that features favorite or ethnic foods.

GRACE BEFORE OR AFTER MEALS

Involve the entire family in writing a special litany of thanksgiving for food. A few examples:

- Work with the alphabet—For apples and bread and chocolate bars and dill, we say: Thank you Lord!

- Use favorite family foods—For pizza with pepperoni and rocky road ice cream, we say: Thank God!

- Identify food with its country of origin—For bananas grown in Colombia and apples from Brazil, and for the people who grew them, picked them, and shipped them, we pray: Thank you Lord.

SCRIPTURE READINGS

Using your family Bible, share with your family one of the following Scripture passages on hunger and justice:

Matthew 25:31–46—I was hungry and you gave me food
Psalm 146:4–9—the Lord is just and feeds the hungry
Isaiah 58:6–12—pour yourself out for the hungry
John 6:1–14 or Mark 8:1–19—Jesus feeds the multitude
Luke 16:19–31—the rich man and Lazarus

FAMILY SHARING

Learn more about how food is grown, produced, and distributed. Discover why some people in our country and world still do not have enough to eat. Some suggestions:

- Keep track, throughout the day, of what you eat and where it comes from in the country or world. Locate the sources of your food on a map or globe. Use an encyclopedia, story book, or video to learn about the people of one of the countries you depend on for the food on your table. Pray for the people of that country during meal time.

- Discuss what it feels like to be hungry for even part of a day. Learn about who the hungry people are in our world, where they live, why they are hungry, and how you can help them as a family. The National Committee for World Food Day (1001 22nd Street NW, Washington DC 20437) provides free background material on World Food Day aimed at helping people better understand food and hunger issues.

FAMILY ACTION RESPONSES

Make World Food Day a day of learning, praying, and doing something about hunger. Try these:

- Add up what your family meals cost during the day and contribute an equal sum to a church or charitable organization that feeds the hungry or provides people with the skills and tools needed to grow their own food.

- Fast for a meal or eat simply for the day, contributing the difference between what you did spend and what you would have spent to an organization that responds to the needs of the hungry.

- Join in a community Crop Walk (sponsored by Church World Services) or other hike for the hungry. Ask friends to pledge money to your family for each kilometer or mile walked.

- Plan a week's meal menu as a family. Try to keep your meal budget at $1.65 or less per person per day—the financial allotment provided to families that receive U.S. Government food stamps. Think about and pray for those for whom this exercise is an ongoing necessity.

- Commit yourselves to eating lower on the food chain. More whole grain products and less red meat. More fresh and less processed foods. Keep track of what this menu costs you as a family. Discuss why people eat as they do, and what options may or may not be open to others.

NOVEMBER

PRAYERS OF REMEMBERING

November is a time for remembering those people, known and unknown, who have made an impact on our lives and history.

Special days immediately come to mind:

ALL SAINTS DAY (November 1)—a day for remembering people from our Christian history whose lives continue to teach us.

ALL SOULS DAY (November 2)—a day for remembering those people who have gone before us and have added to our lives.

VETERANS DAY (November 11)—a day for remembering those people who have represented the ideals of truth, justice and freedom.

This month we join in prayer with and for those who have gone before us. To us death means not decay, but a harvest of memories. Death is not an end; it is the fulfillment of the harvest. Therefore, we come together as a family to remember our roots. We recognize that our lives can become richer by remembering these people through prayer and story during this month.

PREPARATION

Gather saint stories, pictures, statues and/or old family pictures. Place the pictures and a candle in the center of a table.

OPENING SONG

(All sing or recite)
> For all the saints who from hard labor rest,
> 'Who their great faith to all the world confessed,
> Your name, O Jesus, is forever blessed.
> Alleluia, Alleluia!

Leader: God, you have sent many people before us to show us the way to you. Help us to remember together the goodness of their lives.

SCRIPTURE READING

> Dearly beloved, we are God's children now;
> What we shall later be has not yet come to light.
> We know that when it comes to light we shall be like him,
> for we shall see him as he is.
> Everyone who has this hope based on him keeps himself pure,
> as he is pure. (1 John 3:2–3)

REMEMBERING

Invite family members to tell stories of the lives of the saints, especially those saints whose names are in the family. At another or the same gathering invite family members to tell family stories from the old pictures brought to the prayer time. This is a wonderful time to include grandparents. These stories celebrate the goodness of the lives of those who have gone before us.

LITANY OF PRAISE

From the remembering stories, share in a litany of prayer.

Example:	Holy Mary	Pray for us.
	Saint James	Pray for us.
	Grandpa Joe	Pray for us.

OUR FATHER

Join hands around the remembering pictures to pray together in the words of Jesus.

CLOSING PRAYER

Divide the prayer among family members.

>God's reign is for the poor in spirit.
>God's reign is for the humble.
>God's reign is for those who search after justice.
>God's reign is for those who seek peace.
>God's reign is for those who love the poor.

All: Let us ask God to strengthen us so that we too can follow the way of those who have gone before us. Amen.

FEAST OF THANKSGIVING

FAMILY PRAYER SERVICE

Thanksgiving Day is a time when more families come together than any other time during the year. It is a time when families put aside everything else to celebrate their common thankfulness. This prayer service is intended to assist families in celebrating this family time. It may be adapted by any family for its particular needs and circumstances. The prayer service can be used when the family gathers at Thanksgiving or prior to the actual Thanksgiving meal. Other family rituals, such as family songs, remembrances of deceased family members, etc. may be incorporated into the prayer service.

PRAYER

The family and guests stand or sit around the table upon which there is an unlighted candle. A glass of wine or soft drink is at everyone's place. After a few moments in silence, the mother of the family begins.

Mother (or head of household): We come to our table to welcome this feast of Thanksgiving with joy and with gladness. We have prepared this feast with good food and drink. We have gathered together and come around this table to feast and to celebrate the many things for which we are grateful.

Mother (or another): The Lord is our light and our salvation. May this light burn brightly in our hearts and around this table, both at this Thanksgiving and at all of our family meals.

(Grandmother, Grandfather, or oldest child present lights candle.)

Leader: We give thanks today for all the many gifts that we have received.

(Each person is asked to state one thing that he/she is thankful for this Thanksgiving.)

"I am thankful for _____."

Leader: Let us also remember all of those today who are without food and/or a home.

(Pause for silent reflection)

Leader: And let us also remember those members of this family and those loved ones who are not present at our table.

(Either a silent pause or the names of individuals may be said aloud.)

"We remember _____."

BLESSING

(The final prayer is passed around to those children who can read with each child reading one paragraph until the prayer is completed.)

Lord of all blessings,
from you has come a full harvest of gifts to us.
With our uplifted hearts, we come today around this table
to give thanks to you.

We are grateful not only for the gifts of our very lives
but for all the gifts of friendship, love, devotion
and forgiveness that we have shared.

On this Thanksgiving and this day of giving thanks,
we thank you for showing us how to return thanks
by lives of service, by actions of hospitality,
by kindnesses to others, and by concern for each other.

(If there are guests present)

We thank you for the presence of our guest(s) today;
We thank you for (name guests), who,
by their being present in our home,
have added to this feast of joy and celebration.

We are most grateful, today, for the way you, our unseen God,
have become visible to us in one another,

both in our families and our friends, in countless daily
  gifts,
and in the marvels of creation itself.

Father (or oldest member present, while all raise their glasses):

Come, Lord of Gifts.
Bless our table and all the food of this feast.
Let us thank the Lord today and all days.

All Toast: HAPPY THANKSGIVING!

(Conclude with all drinking from their glasses. Begin the meal.)

TABLE DISCUSSION: QUESTIONS/IDEAS

1. What have been the major events of the past year within
    our family and friends?
2. What are some fond memories of Thanksgiving celebra-
    tions from our past?
3. Call or write to those members who cannot be present and
    ask them to write a letter to the family to be read during
    the time between the main course and the dessert.
4. Plan to share photos of special family events.

Part Three

FAMILIES
CELEBRATING
RITUAL
MILESTONES

1

CELEBRATION OF A BIRTHDAY

While each birthday may be considered a rite of passage, some are more universally important than others. For many of us the first significant life transition happened at the age of five or six when we left home to go to school for the first time. At age 13, Jewish children are ushered into adulthood with a formal celebration of Bar/Bat Mitzvah. At age 16, children in most states are considered old enough to become licensed drivers—a first step into adult responsibility for many; and at 18, young women and men become eligible to vote and young men register for the draft. Throughout adulthood, the decade birthdays—30, 40, 50—are important passages for many people, but the 65th birthday—the standard retirement age—is another of the more universal passages in this culture. While all of these are usually happily celebrated occasions, they may also be anxiety-producing passages. These life transitions need to be celebrated for a focus on whatever makes them special, including the new responsibilities they may bring.

SERVICE

(Sign yourself with the sign of the cross and recite this prayer.)

In the name of the Father and of the Son, and of the Holy Spirit. Amen.

God, (I/We) come today to give thanks to you for creating the life of (name). I/We ask your blessing on (name), that he/she may continue to honor and praise you by using the gifts and talents you have given him/her. We ask that (name) continue to grow in age, wisdom, and grace—as Jesus grew.

SCRIPTURE READING

Be thankful. Let the word of Christ dwell in you richly, as in all wisdom you teach and admonish one another, singing psalms, hymns, and spiritual songs with gratitude in your hearts to God. And whatever you do, in word or in deed, do everything in the name of the Lord Jesus, giving thanks to God the Father through him (Colossians 3:15–17).

CLOSING PRAYER

Through baptism, (name) entered God's special life of love. On this special day of remembrance we ask that (name)

—may be faithful to God's love and trust;

—may make good choices in life;

—may continue to grow in age, in wisdom, and in grace as Jesus grew.

(Light candle.)

Let this light symbolize the light of Christ renewing the life of (name).

BLENDED/STEPFAMILY BIRTHDAYS

Birthdays offer opportunities to celebrate the gift of life each person brings to the family or stepfamily unit, and also their uniqueness and personal story.

In stepfamilies, it is not always possible to celebrate birthdays on the actual birth dates themselves, especially when other stepfamilies are involved (other parents, extended family situations). Try to celebrate the birthday of a child or parent on the weekend closest to the actual birth date.

PRIOR TO THE CELEBRATION

Gather all stepfamily members except the birthday person. Brainstorm that person's likes (and dislikes), hobbies, interests, etc. Choose a theme for the party based on the brainstorming. Some possibilities might be: Heavy Metal Madness (13-year old-male), Cincinnati Bengals (9-year-old boy), California Angels (11-year-old boy), Over-the-hill ("mom" at 35), Old Fossil ("dad" at 40).

Consult with the birthday person regarding favorite foods in order to plan the birthday dinner menu and special dessert. Buy decorations pertaining to theme selected and presents.

DAY OF CELEBRATION

One hour before the party, banish the birthday person to his/her room or from the house entirely.

Decorate, wrap presents, cook.

Have the party. Begin with a special prayer for the birthday person (usually one of the other children prepares and prays this).

During the party, try to recall interesting or funny episodes from the birthday person's past, especially those in which the entire stepfamily was involved.

Be sure to take pictures for the stepfamily album.

WEDDING ANNIVERSARY

Use this ritual to celebrate a wedding anniversary, either privately or in the company of friends and family.

Both Partners: In the name of the Father, and of the Son, and of the Holy Spirit. Amen.

PRAYER OF BLESSING AND THANKSGIVING

Recite together: Blessed be the God who has been faithful to us in our journey as married partners and who has shared his mercy with us. We thank you for allowing each of us to be your special gift to the other.

SCRIPTURE READING

Read together: Love is patient, love is kind. Love is not jealous, it is not pompous, it is not inflated, it is not rude, it does not seek its own interests, it is not quick-tempered, it does not brood over injury, it does not rejoice over the wrongdoing but rejoices with the truth. It bears all things, hopes all things, endures all things. Love never fails. (1 Corinthians 13:4–8)

(Spend a few minutes in quiet reflection on God's Word reflecting on the quality of love shared in the marriage relationship and asking God to strengthen the bond between you.)

PRAYER OF HEALING

Pray together: Dear Lord, over this past year we have hurt each other at times. This hurt has caused pain and a wound in our relationship. We ask that you heal these wounds by your presence, and take away the pain of our remembering. Give us the courage to forgive each other as you have forgiven us when we sinned against you. Let us be as gentle and compassionate with one another, as you are with us, as we face this new year. Help us to trust again and to believe in the other person with a realization that the hurting of the other was not done in malice, but out of human weakness and a brokenness of our lives.

RENEWAL OF THE MARRIAGE VOWS

Partners stand, face each other and each holds the hand of the other as he/she takes a turn in the renewal of vows.

I, (name), again pledge my love to you, (name), my wife/husband.

I promise to be true to you in good times in bad, in sickness and in health.

I will love you and honor you all the days of my life.

Each signs the other with the sign of the cross and offers an embrace of peace.

CONCLUDING PRAYER

Recite together:

Lord, may we both praise you when we are happy and turn to you in our sorrows.

Lord, may we be glad that you help us in our work and know that you are with us in our need.

Lord, may we pray to you in the community of the Church and be your witnesses in the world.

Lord, may we reach old age in the company of our family and friends and come at last to the kingdom of heaven.

Amen.

(Light candle) Let this light symbolize our hope in tomorrow and in our eternal life together.

GRADUATION

Because graduation is the culmination of so much that is intensely personal, one family invented a tradition that has become significant for them, the personal diploma.

The personal diploma began as something to complement the institutional diploma received by an 18-year-old son. In contrast to the somber black lettering on white parchment, this diploma is elaborately decorated with a colorful and intricate border that appeared at first to be a fruit-and-flower design but, on closer inspection, actually was interspersed with footballs, football helmets, and baseball mitts.

The text, done in calligraphy, was long and personal. It celebrated four years of high school, including adolescent compulsions, successes, and failures. It touched on such things as driving, dating, and working, as well as math, music, English literature, sports, and special family times.

Naturally, each graduate would deserve different commemorative details. This is how theirs began:

To our son _____ on his graduation on this, the 5th day of June, 19___, we present this diploma in honor of four rich and sometimes arduous years at _____ High School.

As you collect this diploma and move on to the next stage of your development, we, your loving and proud parents, remember the vivid moments of these important years...

The parents wrote the text themselves and found a local artist to design their diploma. It is beautifully framed and now hangs in their son's room at college. This tradition is just the kind of personal and creative response that produces the warmth and satisfaction and pleasure we all want in our families.

Incorporate Scripture, prayer, and story telling into your family graduation celebration.

Scripture: Ecclesiastes 3:1–8 reminds us there is a time for everything—and that God is with us in all seasons. It can serve as a reminder of God's ongoing presence in the midst of change.

Prayer: Develop a special family prayer that expresses your thanks and/or your hopes for your graduating son or daughter, or use the following:

Parent/Leader:

(Name) you are a unique creation,
a person blessed by God with life,
a person called, in love, to grow
and to share your gifts with others.

We come together today to celebrate your accomplishments,
to reflect on who you are for us,
and to share our dreams for your future.

May your graduation day be filled with happiness and joy.

We rejoice in who you are for us as a family, calling to mind especially your gifts of _____ and _____.

(Family members can be invited to share comments and stories here that speak of the uniqueness and giftedness of the graduate)

May God continue to bless you and challenge you.
May you always be surrounded by people who support and love you.
May you grow more fully into the man/woman that God wants you to be, and that the world so desperately needs.

We ask this today, in hope and expectation that God will continue the great things already begun in you.

Amen.

5

AT HOME CELEBRATION WHEN A CHILD MARRIES

OPENING PRAYER

Loving God, you understand the hearts of all your children. Look with love upon us as we come before you, not without concern, but with great joy, for (name) is about to leave our home.

As a gift to us, he/she came into our family; as a gift to all he/she shall meet, we send him/her in your care to your greater family, to all your children in our world. We thank you, the Giver, for the hours we have shared together, and for the times of still warmer joy—yet unknown, but sure to come.

But this, Gracious One, is the time of action, the day of light for his/her forthcoming marriage. Together then, we pray now for your child, our son/daughter (name).

READINGS

A sibling or parent does the reading.

> Reading 1: Ephesians 3:14–21 or Colossians 3:12–17 or reading of your choice from St. Paul's Letters
> Reading 2: John 17:20–23 or Matthew 5:13–16 or Gospel of your choice.

HOMILY

Parents (and if they wish, siblings) write the homily. Suggestions to include:

> Qualities of child being married
> Ways this child has impacted the family
> Forgiveness for hurts committed and omissions
> Ask for forgiveness of times we have hurt child
> Welcome of fiancé(e)

Mention this is time of transition, change—support and love will follow them as they form their own family

INTERCESSIONS

For all parents and children, that they may share in the love of God through their love of each other, we pray...

For all families suffering hurt and rejection, that they may seek forgiveness and once again be connected, we pray...

For the hungry, the homeless, the sick in heart as well as body, that they may find shelter and warmth, we pray...

For [child and fiancé(e)], that they may grow in wisdom and understanding and experience the friendship of each other and Jesus, we pray...

For [fiancé(e)'s family], that the love they share may reflect the love of the Trinity, we pray...

Additional prayers can be written by family members.

BLESSING

Father: Lord our God, be with us now as we pray. Look with favor upon this our son/daughter (name), for whom his/her wedding day will be most special. We, his/her parents, together with all his family, surround him/her with our love and prayer as he/she prepares to marry (name).

Mother: My son/daughter and child of my womb, your wedding day indeed will be mostly special to you, one that you will long remember. We, your family, are grateful that we are able to share it with you and are able to support you with our prayers and love.

Father: Blessed are you, Lord our God, who has graced our son/daughter with life and health so that he/she might reach this day. You have blessed him/her abundantly over the years and have carefully prepared him/her for this important step in his/her life.

Lord, our God, bring together and unite all our prayers, our hopes, and love into a single blessing for him/her.

Amen.

WEDDING BLESSING

Father or Mother: (Name) and (name), we pray that you will treat adversity as a common enemy and will not try to bear it alone and silently;
That you will not strive to be the strongest but to be strong together;
That you will recognize each other's strengths and nourish them;
That you will know each other's weaknesses and never use them;
That your vows will not bind you but bond you;
That you will love and care more for the other than for anything;
That you will love and care for your children;
That in the end, you will have known more joy and happiness than you have known pain and sorrow.
May your path be smooth and straight.

Mother:

As you give this blessing, place your hands on the couple.
(Name of child), may the Lord who gave you into our care and made you a joy to our home bless and keep you.

[Fiancé(e)'s name], may the Lord, who turns the hearts of parents to their children and the hearts of children to their parents, smile on you and be kind to you.

Father:

As you give this blessing, place your hands on the couple.
(Name) and (name), may the Lord, who delights in our love for one another, turn toward you and give you peace.

May the God of love and peace abide in you, guide your steps, and confirm your heart in his love, now and forever. Amen.

6

CELEBRATING RETIREMENT:
A FAMILY RITUAL

Most retirement ceremonies point to the accomplishments of the honoree and look forward to the positive side of retirement. Somewhere—in the family and/or in the religious community—there need to be rites that anticipate the joys *and* the sorrows of the next phase of life. Rites are needed that celebrate the new relationship with the rest of the family and community and call attention to family and community responsibilities in this new relationship.

As is the case in all passages, more than the individual is involved. Retirement is not only a passage for the individual but for the surrounding family and community as well. The following celebration offers an opportunity for family and friends to join with the retiree in looking back to the accomplishments of the past and forward to the new opportunities provided by retirement.

PREPARATION

Prior to the ceremony, invite family and friends of the retiree to gather photos and recall stories (both serious and humorous) that speak of the role he or she has played in the life of his or her family, friends, and local community.

GREETING

Leader: Dear friends, we gather today (tonight) to recognize (Name) and celebrate an important time of passage in his/her life—a time of passage through retirement to redirection. As we begin our celebration, let us call to mind God's special presence to us in times of celebration:

Dear God, you are mother and father to all; you defend, nurture, and support us as we seek to serve you. You strengthen us in moments of pain and celebrate with us in times of joy. We thank you in a special way today (tonight) for (Name). We recognize the many ways he/she has served you and others in his/her business, professional, and family lives. We celebrate (Name)'s retirement, confident that it will be for him/her a time of continued growth, service, and renewal in faith. Be with us, loving God, in our celebration.

SCRIPTURE

You can use Ecclesiastes 3:1–8 (God is with us in all the seasons of our life) or 2 Corinthians 9:10–15 (the service you have given brings glory to God) or another Scripture reading which suits the occasion.

INVITATION TO SHARING

Leader: We come together to recognize (Name)—to toast, roast and boast of what (Name) has been, and continues to be for us. This is a time for sharing stories, both serious and hilarious. I invite you now to share who (Name) is for you and what you have learned about the values that make him/her who he/she is.

LITANY OF BLESSING

Ask all gathered to extend their hands in blessing toward (Name) as the following petitions are read by family and friends. Invite them to respond with a resounding Amen! to each prayer of blessing.

1. (Name), we thank you for the many ways that you have touched our lives in the past. May your supportive presence be with us for many years to come. Amen!

2. We thank God for the gift you have been to your family. May you continue to share your faith and love with us, reminding us about who we are as a family and as children of God. Amen!

3. We celebrate together your many accomplishments and contributions to our community. May we continue to be enriched by your experience and knowledge. Amen!

4. We thank God for the direction your life has taken. May God bless you with new directions, new insights, and new opportunities for sharing your gifts with others. Amen!

5. Finally we pledge to you our continued love and support as you enter this time of change and transition. May your troubles be small and your circle of friends large. May you continue to grow in your friendship with God and share God's love with all you meet. Amen!

7

WAKE SERVICE: DEATH
IN THE FAMILY

The death of a family member can be a time of deep sorrow. When this passage is ritualized in a meaningful way, involving family members, it becomes easier to recognize both the pain and the joy that are present. People are able to express themselves and feel part of the experience. The ritual makes the experience personal and healing.

TABLE OF REMEMBRANCE

A Table of Remembrance set up at the funeral home for the wake service encourages family members and friends to remember and share stories about the deceased. Each family member brings a picture, object, or some other token that evokes a memory of the deceased. During the wake service, family members are invited to share their memory or story with the family and friends gathered.

One story usually sparks other ideas or stories, weaving a rich tapestry of remembrance, and changes the dynamics at the funeral home. Instead of sitting passively, visitors often pay their respects at the casket, and then gather at the table. They pick up the objects, pictures and mementos, and tell stories, each from his or her own perspective. This sets the tone for the wake service, one of story telling and warm memories.

WAKE SERVICE

The wake service and funeral liturgy should involve as many family members as possible. For an older person, the pall bearers might be grandchildren representing different families, including granddaughters. Adult children may bless the casket and cover it with the pall, grandchildren may be readers and gift bearers at the liturgy. Others may be Eucharistic ministers.

Call to Worship

Leader: May the God of hope give you the fullness of peace, and may the Lord of life be always with you.

All: And also with you.

Opening Song: "Prayer of St. Francis"

Leader: We gather this evening to remember (name). We pray for him/her and for us gathered, that we may know God's peace.

First Reading: 2 Corinthians 5:1, 6-10

Responsorial: Psalm 27

Gospel Reading: John 16:20-22

Reflections/Family Stories

Invite those who would like to share a story or a memory of the deceased to come forward at this time. You may wish to identify several family members in advance who plan to take part in this sharing. Their stories may involve objects, photos, etc. from the Table of Remembrance.

Prayer of Intercession

Leader: Let us turn to Christ Jesus with confidence and faith in the power of his cross and resurrection:

Leader: Risen Lord, pattern of our life for ever: Lord, have mercy.

All: Lord, have mercy.

Leader: Promise and image of what we shall be: Lord, have mercy.

All: Lord, have mercy.

Leader: Lord Jesus, gentle Shepherd who brings rest to our souls, give peace to (name) for ever: Lord, have mercy.

All: Lord, have mercy.

(All recite together)

> *Our Father*
> *Hail Mary*

Leader: Loving God, we thank you for (name) who was so dear
and beloved to us. We thank you that through his/her life
and suffering, he/she became a person we all could love.
We pray that all whom (name) held dear will be remem-
bered and honored by those who come after him/her. We
ask that his/her special gifts will continue to be valued by
us long after her death. We pray that nothing of (name's)
life will be lost, but that his/her spirt will remain in our
hearts and give strength to us in our times of need. We
thank you, God, that the life-giving spirit and presence of
(name) will go on living in our hearts, our minds, and in
our lives.

Blessing

Closing Song

8

REMEMBERING THE DEATH OF A LOVED ONE (FAMILY MEMBER OR FRIEND)

(*Light candle*) Let this light symbolize my/our hope in tomorrow and in the eternal life promised by Jesus.

In the name of the Father, and of the Son,
and of the Holy Spirit. Amen.

God of our ancestors in faith,
by the covenant made on Mt. Sinai
you taught your people to strengthen the bonds of family
    and friendship through faith, hope, and love.
Today I/we remember the eternal covenant you made with
    (name). I/we come to give thanks for the life of (Name)
    and to pray for peace until we are once again united in
    your eternal love.

SCRIPTURE READING

"Do not let your hearts be troubled. You have faith in God; have faith also in me. In my Father's house there are many dwelling places. If there were not, would I have told you that I am going to prepare a place for you? And if I go and prepare a place for you, I will come back again and take you to myself, so that where I am you also may be. Where I am going you know the way." Thomas said to him, "Master, we do not know where you are going; how can we know the way?" Jesus said to him, "I am the way and the truth and the life. No one comes to the Father except through me." (John 14: 1–6)

Reflect privately in thanksgiving for the life of (name). Recall both the moments of joy and sadness that you shared together. Ask God to heal any hurt you experienced with (name) so you can be free to live life in a fuller way. Ask God to bless you as you continue your life journey without (name).

CONCLUDING PRAYER

God, (name), has entered your eternal life and has left behind those who have loved him/her. Grant that I/we may hold (name's) memory in my/our heart(s), with hope that we will be brought together again in your divine love. Amen.

Part Four

FAMILIES CELEBRATING ETHNIC RITUALS AND TRADITIONS

1

RECLAIMING ETHNIC CULTURE AND TRADITIONS

Along with food and affection, parents pass on to young children a vision of life. That vision helps children gain a sense of who they are as individuals and as family, and of what the world is like. It helps young people make sense of their lives and provides a foundation for all later learnings about life as a man or woman, how people should interact, and what values are worth living out. This vision of life is often referred to as "culture." Often, as parents struggle to articulate the vision of life they want to share with their children, they realize that many of the values they themselves hold were passed on through family and ethnic traditions. Behind simple family stories, ethnic customs, and national celebrations lies a vision of life. Reclaiming ethnic traditions as a family provides a way of claiming the values we live by and celebrating our connectedness with family members who came before. It provides a way of celebrating our values not just in words, but also in food and decor, song and dance.

SUGGESTIONS FOR RECLAIMING ETHNIC TRADITIONS

1.   Explore your family history. Talk with older family members about where your family came from and when it settled where it did. What families or ethnic groups came together to make you who you are? Who were the saints, sinners, and story tellers in your family's past? What were their jobs and hobbies, accomplishments and adventures?

2.   Connect with family values and traditions. Talk with older family members about the values passed on to them by their families. Ask about the events they celebrated growing

up, and how they celebrated them. Were any celebrations unique to their family or ethnic group? What made the celebrations unique—the event being celebrated or the way in which it was done? Are any of the older traditions still alive in your family? Is anyone willing to pass on how and why they are done?

3.   Explore ethnic traditions and celebrations. Borrow a book or video from the library that details the history and traditions of people from your ethnic culture. Contact groups in your area (church and civic) that may continue to celebrate the traditions of your ethnic culture; see if there is an upcoming event in which you can participate as a family.

4.   Choose an ethnic tradition or celebration that you would like to reclaim as a family, adapting it as needed. Invite members of your extended family or friends to join in the celebration. If, like many Americans, your family represents several ethnic or national groups, find a way of recognizing each. Start small, adding new components to your family celebration each year.

5.   As ethnic celebrations become traditions in your family, share with your children why you celebrate as you do. Help them to claim the values of their ethnic culture and connect with their history.

2

PASSING ON CULTURAL TRADITIONS

ROSIE PIÑA

What is it like to almost lose your culture, realize it just in time and begin a re-entry phase into your culture? Well, it is sad, exciting and challenging—in that order! I suppose our story is repeated many times by those who come to this realization and go to work to "correct mistakes."

One of the first things we become aware of is what we have lost in the way of cultural traditions. Depending upon how meaningful and important they had been, we find ourselves attempting to retrieve them and make them a part of our lives again.

How can we have fun while passing on cultural traditions? If you are Hispanic and live in San Antonio, Texas, it really isn't that hard because you have a lot of help in the cultural environment of this city.

One fun thing that brings us in touch with our culture is a trip down to Market Square where you feel like you are in Mexico. Mexican culture pervades the shops, foods, and entertainment. Hand in hand with Market Square is the definite Mexican influence of our River Walk and other downtown attractions, such as La Villita. Again, the shops, foods and crafts displayed here all speak to us of our rich Mexican heritage.

We consider it fun also to attend Mass at San Fernando Cathedral. The old building itself resounds with what we know of the Spanish missionaries who founded it. But it truly comes alive during the Holy Mass celebrated in Spanish with a Mariachi choir leading the sung parts of the Mass, accompanied by guitaras, maracas, trompetas, and violines. The cathedral's four corners are brightly lit with the veladoras that the faithful place there daily. These tall votive candles give us an

opportunity to tell our children of the deep faith and devotion
of the Mexican/Mexican-American people, a cultural strength
that we want to pass on and preserve for all generations.
Several of the many missions in this area are also active
parishes and cultural traditions can be seen and felt there too.

Are there similar cultural experiences in the city where
you live? When was the last time you were there?

Birthday parties and holiday celebrations also include
some of our cultural traditions. A piñata is used during many
of these celebrations and is both a fun thing and a teaching
tool. The piñata is a bamboo-framed object, made in a variety
of shapes, covered with brightly colored paper and filled with
candies. The piñata is usually hung over a tree branch so that
guests at the party can strike it with a stick to break it open
and release the candies. Originally, the piñata was made in
"devil" shapes and signified the evil in the world. The stick
represented virtue. The blindfolded person struck at the "evil"
with the stick of virtue, receiving "advice" from all the by-
standers yelling out the position of the piñata (up, down, on
your left, etc.) This signified that one goes through life blindly
with many "voices" giving direction; some are right and some
are wrong. When one did connect with the piñata and broke
it, all the candies were released and fell to the ground. These
were said to be God's graces falling on the earth, blessing the
place where they fell.

During the re-entry phase I spoke of at the beginning, we
realized that a very meaningful tradition had been almost lost
to our family. This tradition was the "Posadas," a re-enactment
of Mary and Joseph seeking a place to stay in Bethlehem
where they were finally given a stable in which to sleep and
where Jesus was born. Originally, the posadas were held over
a period of nine nights. Each night, several families would
gather and go to one home seeking a place to stay, only to be
denied. This would be repeated each night until finally the
last night they were accepted at the "inn" and a big fiesta
would follow. The translated version that we follow now is to
gather and go to at least three or four homes in one night and
at the last home Mary and Joseph are "accepted" at the "inn,"
and that is where we hold the big fiesta. It's more fun if you

have children whom you can dress up as Mary and Joseph, and even more fun if you can get a real donkey!

What is one of your holiday cultural traditions? Is it practiced in its original form or has it been adapted to today's reality?

One of our festive cultural traditions is the celebration of a "Quinceañera." When a young lady celebrates her 15th birthday, a big celebration is planned. There is always a Mass of Thanksgiving and usually a big reception and dance. The young lady is "attended" by a court of 14 friends and their escorts. Much is done to observe the cultural and spiritual significance of this occasion because the root of this celebration is to thank God for the young lady's life up to now and to consecrate her as she enters womanhood, praying for God's graces to continue to be with her during this very important time of her life.

Other meaningful events in our lives are also fun ways of sharing and reflecting on cultural traditions. Our weddings are fun-filled festive occasions. In the wedding ceremony, there are two elements which are cultural traditions: the lazo, usually made of beads in the shape of a rosary with two loops which is placed around the bride and groom to "unite" them; and the aras, which are 13 coins that the bride and groom exchange signifying their commitment to provide for the material needs of each other and their home. At weddings a lot of fun is provided simply by reuniting many relatives that you seldom see. Trying to identify and follow the family lineage is an adventure in itself! The wedding celebration ends with another very beautiful cultural tradition. Before the bride and groom leave on their honeymoon, the grandparents and parents give them their blessing as they kneel before them and all the other wedding guests.

Are there some special cultural traditions at your celebrations? Are there some that have been lost that you would like to bring back?

Vacations can be fun and culture-enriching as well. One that we will never forget is a motor trip that our extended family took to Mexico. It was the first time into Mexico for our teenage children and of course one of the main cultural enrichments that we were seeking was the Spanish language. More significant was that this vacation originated with our desire to make a pilgrimage to the Basilica of Our Lady of Guadalupe, a cultural/faith tradition.

The purpose of the pilgrimage was so that the whole family could pray for our youngest nephew, Jesusito, who is a physically challenged child. Jesusito was three years old and could not walk due to cerebral palsy. The fun part was getting Grandma Josie, Grandpa Joe, Uncle Tito, Aunt Molly, cousins David, Danny, Dennis, our daughter, Tisha, Roberto and I, and Jesusito, of course, and luggage, into one Suburban! It was fun...really it was! The trip gave us an opportunity to see the beauty of our mother country, meet many of its people, and enjoy being Mexican-Americans in Mexico.

Have you ever had the opportunity to visit your "mother" land? Do you still know the language?

THE HOME ALTAR

The home altar is a longstanding tradition in families of Mexican origin. The altar is usually a simple affair, set up in a nook in the family room or master bedroom. There is usually a predominant statue of Mary or Christ in one of their manifestations, frequently attended by other saints. More often than not there are flowers and votive candles on the altar. The dynamics of encounter in the devotion take the form of prayer, usually of petition and/or thanksgiving. Favors are requested and gratitude is expressed for favors granted. The sense of sacred space and ritual activity is quite evident. Jesus, Mary, and the saints, in their various manifestations, generally express the primary concern of the practitioners: Mary in her pivotal role of mediatrix with God; Jesus in his human dimension, such as the Sacred Heart, symbolizing love and compassion; St. Jude as patron of the impossible; St. Anthony of Padua as patron of lost articles, and so forth. The overriding sense of the existence of the home altar is the manifestation of the divine presence in the home. God is there for his people.

LAS POSADAS, NAVIDAD, DÍA DE LOS TRES REYES

The Christmas throughout most of Latin America is a season of bright flowers and brilliant nights. Though Central America is entering winter at this time of year, the weather is warm and dry for the most part, and in those countries in the Southern Hemisphere summer is just beginning. The celebrations, the holiday foods, the songs, though they vary from country to country according to the influence of each country's indigenous Indians, all share a strong Latin heritage dating from the arrival of Roman Catholicism 400 years ago. Christmas is, then, very much a religious holiday centered around the age-old story of the Nacimiento, Christ's birth. Here we focus on Mexico and Venezuela to describe some typical festivities commemorating this most important holiday.

POSADAS

In Mexico, the joyful observances begin on December 16th. From that evening until the eve of Christmas, processions of family and friends go from house to house, by prearranged invitation, to take part in one or another of the countless *posadas*, or "lodging" parties, that provide the central social events of the season. Part amateur theatre, part religious ceremony, the *posadas* dramatize the nine-day journey of Mary and Joseph to Bethlehem.

In preparation for the season of *posadas*, the people of Mexico decorate their houses and apartments with festoons of greenery and build small altars atop which they place tiny nativity scenes representing the creche, the stable, the shepherds, their flocks, and the expectant Mary and Joseph. Then, just as evening falls, the members of each *posada* gather to recreate the ancient pilgrimage. Two children, carrying figures of Mary and Joseph, lead the procession. In towns the throng may go from house to house, but in cities they may wind through apartment house corridors or even from room to room. At each door, they pause to sing that they are tired and cold and in need of shelter for the night. They ask for lodging.

Other members of the *posada* take the role of inhospitable innkeepers. Opening the door just a crack, they refuse to take in the strangers, and the party moves on. Finally, they reach the door of the evening's host's house. When Joseph identifies himself and tells of his family's long journey and of the imminent birth, the owners respond, also in song, saying, in effect, "Then you are welcome in our humble home, and may the Lord remember us all when our souls go to heaven!"

The ritual is by now a very old one, and though every adult has repeated it a great many times, each *posada* holds mystery and excitement. When at last the pilgrims are invited in, a great cheer goes up. The candlelit procession enters and gathers around the decorated altar to kneel reverently in prayer. Then the evening's fun begins. Fireworks, delicious sweets and fruits, dancing and a *piñata* filled with small treats for the children are traditional ingredients of the party.

The *posadas* are repeated for nine evenings, the last on Christmas Eve. This evening of joyous climax is the most solemn and elaborate of them all. For the first time, two members of the procession step forward as "godparents." They carry a figure of the Baby Jesus, which they lay gently in the manger. Other participants light candles set in a row around the altar, and everyone joins in singing hosannas.

Christmas Eve ends with the *Misa de Gallo*, or Mass of the Cock, at midnight. After the service, everyone spills out into the streets, fireworks explode overhead, bells ring, and a joyous clamor sounds all over town. In some communities a special parade, with floats and *tableaux vivants* representing biblical scenes, provides a spectacular finale to the public part of Christmas. Finally, in what is more often than not the middle of the night, everyone returns home for a special dinner.

December 25th is typically a quiet family day, which is understandable—after the very late night that has just passed.

In the days that follow Mexicans continue the joyous season by attending special bullfights, *pastores* (miracle plays), and fiestas. December 28th is the day of *Los Santos Inocentes* (Holy Innocents), a time for children to play practical jokes and tricks.

NACIMIENTOS/PESEBRES

In Venezuela, *posadas* are not traditional, but the season begins, nevertheless, on December 16th when families bring their *nacimientos*, more often called *pesebres* here, out of safekeeping and arrange them in the most prominent part of the living room. Venezuelan *pesebres* range from the most literal depictions of the nativity scene to some rather unorthodox displays that combine modern-day electric trains and cartoon figures with the traditional shepherds, pilgrims, Wise Men, and the Holy Family.

Going to one or more of the nine *Misas de Aguinaldo*, the 4:30 a.m. Christmas carol services, is a bracing custom that most Venezuelans observe. Firecrackers explode and bells ring to call worshipers from bed in the predawn hours. *Aguinaldo* is the Venezuelan term both for a carol and for a gift, which gives some notion of the spirit in which the joyous singers lift their voices to the Niño. The last of the Christmas Masses takes place on *Nochebuena de Navidad*, Christmas Eve. Families go together to the late night *Misa de Gallo* and then home to a huge and fancy dinner.

The Day of the Holy Innocents, December 28th, is marked much as it is in Mexico as a day for playing jokes on friends. It is also the day on which the Church recalls the martyrdom of the young children who were slain by Herod in retribution for Christ's birth.

DÍA DE LOS TRES REYES

Gift giving does not occur until January 6th, the *Día de los Tres Reyes*, Three Kings Day, when the Magi are said to return and to give presents to children, as they once did to El Niño Jesus. Just to be sure that they do not escape notice, many children prepare for this night by writing letters to the Magi, listing their good deeds and suggesting gifts that they hope to receive. When children awaken on the morning of the 6th they find the straw left the night before by their beds gone and gifts delivered in its place. This, they know, is the work of the Magi and their hungry camels.

THE FEAST OF
ST. JOHN THE BAPTIST

The feast of St. John the Baptist on June 24th has always been one of the favorites in all of Latin America, the Philippines, Spain, Mexico, and Hispanic United States. Puerto Ricans make a particular festive celebration of this date because San Juan is the patron of the namesake capital city of the Island. Early in the morning, wherever possible, people go to beaches and rivers to welcome the day with the ablutions of St. John. During the day, in many places, people have fun "baptizing" passersby in the streets. This is in accord with the proverb which says, *"En el día de San Juan, toda aguas es Jordan"* (On the day of St. John, all water is Jordan water). It is also customary on that day to welcome Summer with *luminarias* and bonfires.

KWANZAA

Beginning on December 26th, many African Americans celebrate Kwanzaa, a holiday that originated in the United States at the height of the civil rights movement in the 1960s, and commemorate their African heritage. Created out of rituals borrowed from African harvest festivals, and using the language of Swahili to designate its symbols and customs, Kwanzaa continues for a week, during which participants gather with family and friends to exchange gifts and to light a series of black, red, and green candles symbolizing the seven basic values of African American family life—unity, self-determination, collective work and responsibility, cooperative economics, purpose, creativity, and faith.

In the days just before the start of Kwanzaa, the whole family joins in decorating the house with all manner of black, red, and green paper decorations. Some families also hang homemade ornaments on an evergreen "Kwanzaa bush." A principal point of the holiday is to educate children about their heritage, and many households seize the day to display African artwork and in other ways pay tribute to Africa, past and present. They also set out photographs of recent generations of the family. The mother of the family sets a ceremonial table, placing on it an ear of corn to symbolize each of her children, and a carved and decorated unity cup, or *kikombe*, with which toasts will be made each evening.

Then, on seven consecutive nights beginning with December 26th, the family gathers to light the *kinara*, or seven-holed candleholder. On the first night one of the children is asked to light the central—black—candle, symbolizing unity, after which the parents talk about the meaning of the word. On the next night someone lights a red one, to represent self-determination, and so on through the seven nights. Each night the parents lead the family in talking about what the evening's central idea means to each person in the room.

And each night, everyone also drinks from the unity cup which is filled with a *tambico*, or libation; as it passes around the table, parents reminisce about members of the family, saluting especially those whose lives may be in some way inspirational.

December 31st is the night for the giving of *zawadi*, or gifts, mostly to the children. The gifts traditionally include a book and a heritage symbol, such as an African art object, and something homemade. A Kwanzaa slogan, "You must achieve to receive," is taken very seriously in some families, who reward their children in direct proportion to their accomplishments. Other households, particularly those that do not also celebrate Christmas, exercise much more latitude in giving to youngsters, and the usual sorts of toys, games, and dolls are likely to turn up amongst the *zawadi*. The seven-day celebration ends later in the evening with a feast. It's a happy time with many friends and family gathered together, a table set lavishly with African and African American foods, and plenty of music—usually a mix of African American and African sounds. When everyone has finished eating, they rise together, recommit themselves to the seven principles of Kwanzaa, and bid each other happy months ahead. The host ends the formal part of the party with the wish that "at the end of this year, may we sit again together, in larger number, with greater achievement...and a higher level of human life."

7

LUCIA DAY

Swedes consider their Christmas season to begin late in November on the first Sunday in Advent, when churches and many households light the first of four Advent candles. But it is on December 13th, Luciadagen (Lucia Day), that the holiday pace quickens noticeably.

The Lucia for whom this day is named was, according to the most widely accepted legend, a Sicilian Christian who was condemned to death in A.D. 304 for her faith. She supposedly ran afoul of her fiance's family when she chose to give her dowry to the people of a poverty-stricken village rather than to her in-laws. The prospective groom, deciding that such outrageous behavior could only mean that his intended was afflicted with Christianity, reported her to the Roman prefect. She was condemned to burn; but although flames enveloped her pyre, she herself was unharmed. Only when one of her captors plunged his sword through Lucia did she finally die.

This anniversary, which was one of hundreds of feast days subsequently celebrated by Christians everywhere during the year, took on unique significance in the western parts of Sweden during the Middle Ages. One year in early December when a terrible famine gripped the land, Lucia appeared to a Swedish peasant. In his vision Lucia was robed in white, crowned with a circle of lights, bearing gifts of food. This miraculous event was interpreted as an omen of future prosperity, and its celebration coincided with an already long-standing belief that the Norse goddess Freya appeared at about this time each year—the time of the winter solstice—to confer her blessing on the land. The two traditions joined and strengthened each other.

Luciadagen remained a festival of the western provinces, marked by certain rituals associated with the solstice, until the late 19th century, when the custom of the eldest girl in the family dressing up to impersonate Lucia first developed. It became a semi-official holiday in this century, one celebrated both within the family and in many shops, offices, clubs, and factories, beginning in the 1920s.

CELEBRATION

Early on the morning of December 13th, Lucia, Queen of Lights, appears in her parents' bedroom, dressed in white and wearing on her head a crown of green foliage and lighted candles. As she carries a tray of special buns and hot coffee, she sings the famed old Neapolitan song "Santa Lucia," only in triple time and with Swedish words. One popular version of the song, to which there are many variations, begins "Mute was the night with gloom: Now hear faint bustling In every silent room, Like pinions rustling, Lo! on our threshold there, White-clad, with flame-crowned hair, Sancta Lucia, Sancta Lucia."

If the family's Lucia has younger sisters, they may follow her, also dressed in white, as though they are her attending angels. Occasionally younger brothers dress up as "star boys" and join in, too, though this again is something of a recent custom. The star boys, who also dress in white robes but wear pointed hats and carry star-topped wands or staves, seem to derive from a different tradition, albeit one also associated with Christmas. Beginning sometime in the Middle Ages, groups of young men, usually students, paraded in costume through the streets singing carols and putting on biblical plays. Often the populace rewarded their efforts with money, food, and drink, which resulted in such giddy and unruly parties that the authorities eventually saw fit to prohibit the young men's activities. Today's star boys appear to be the well-behaved descendants of those earlier mischief-makers.

After the early morning celebration of Luciadagen, Swedes go off to jobs and schools where they continue the day's festivities. In large offices and factories, as well as in shopping centers, it is now customary to elect a young girl to play Lucia, and she passes among her fellow workers bestowing coffee and buns during the morning. Towns and even cities elect their own Lucia, and in Stockholm, where the Nobel Prize winners are usually named on or just before this day, she has the semi-official duty of crowning the winner of the literature prize in formal ceremonies at City Hall. In many places Lucia ends her nameday by leading a candlelight parade through the streets.

8

WIGILIA

The Poles have always combined religious and family closeness at Christmas time. Gift giving plays only a minor role in the joyous rituals, emphasis being placed instead on making special foods and decorations that capture everyone's attention as young and old prepare for the season. The climactic event is the Wigilia (Feast of Vigil), celebrated in the home on Christmas Eve.

The Wigilia, which derives its name from the Latin word *vigilare* (to watch or keep vigil), has since Christian times been observed as a time of joyful waiting, commemorating the vigil that shepherds kept on the night of Christ's birth. But historians trace its origins to an even earlier age when Poles observed the winter solstice about this time of year. In pre-Christian folklore, the god Saturn conquered darkness and restored the sun, and because he also represented fairness and justice, part of the ancient observance involved people showing forgiveness to one another and sharing foods. Two thousand years and more later, Poles pay homage to this ancient tradition in the *Gody*, the days of harmony and good will that commence at the Wigilia and last until Epiphany, January 6th.

In many families vestiges of ancient beliefs are apparent also in the custom of making the house uncommonly hospitable at this season. According to legend, wandering spirits roam the land during the darkest days and, just in case there is some truth in the tale, people make provision for the comfort of these lost souls. They leave out a pan of warm water and a bowl of nuts and fruits to refresh possible visitors from the spirit world; and they put away knives and scissors lest the wanderers injure themselves.

CELEBRATION AND FEASTING

The Wigilia meal itself involves rituals that have been handed down over many centuries. Though each region of the country has developed its own unique practices, there is a fundamental similarity among them that derives from the influence of the Catholic Church.

The Wigilia begins officially with the announcement of the first star of the evening. A candle placed at the window for the Christ Child is lighted, and the family assembles to share the feast. By tradition, the table is surrounded by an odd number of chairs, including one for the Baby Jesus. The table, already set, has a bed of straw laid under the white table linen to remind everyone of the straw-filled manger in Bethlehem. On a plate, with money under it to signify a prosperous future, are the symbolic bread and salt without which no household can exist. In the corners of the room are sheaves of golden grain, a silent prayer that the coming year's harvest will be bountiful.

The meal opens with the ritual breaking and sharing of the *Oplatek*, a large unleavened wafer that has been stamped with scenes of the Nativity and blessed by the parish priest. First the parents break the wafer and share it with one another, embracing and exchanging the message of love. Then mother and father break their pieces again with other members of the family, expressing as they do so the mutual commitment of one for all and all for one. (Family members who are far away will receive pieces of *Oplatek* by mail—a gesture of continuing family communion.)

The dishes served are also prescribed by custom. They must be meatless in observance of the feast day, and often they number 12, to symbolize the Twelve Apostles. Ideally, they are prepared with ingredients harvested from the region's own fields, orchards, gardens, woods, and rivers. A clear beet soup filled with mushrooms is the favorite first course, followed by carp and perhaps several other sort of fish dishes as well as several winter vegetables. Pastries with meatless fillings are traditional, too, including the dumplinglike *pierozhki*. A grain pudding called *kutya* always appears, though, with so many delicious alternatives, its eating is more a matter of symbolism than pleasure: ingredients include peeled grain mills to grind grain; honey, to sweeten the days' labors; and poppy seed, to insure a peaceful sleep. The Wigilia concludes with poppy-seed cake and a compote of 12 fruits, again in honor of the Apostles.

When all have finished, the replete diners rise together and regroup around the Christmas tree where simple, often handmade, gifts await everyone. Midnight finds many families at the *Pasterka*, the Shepherds' Mass. The next day, Christmas, is spent in the company of close family. Christmas dinner's main course is usually a large ham, Polish sausages, or perhaps the traditional hunter's stew, called *bigos*, prepared, as its name suggests, from wild game. More traditional Polish communities also celebrate December 26th, "the Second Day of Christmas," in commemoration of the life of St. Stephen. Church services, family visiting, and special meals mark this day, too. Some Poles exchange blessings by tossing a handful of rice at one another, recalling as they do the stoning of the martyred saint.

Part Five

FAMILIES CELEBRATING RITUALS THROUGH THE DAY

Introduction

In considering the daily events of our lives there are many moments of ritual which go unnoticed. These moments contain the elements of movement, words, and symbols which are present in all rituals. It is the ordinary nature of these moments which make it difficult for us to view them as rituals.

In most 24-hour periods lie a treasure of rituals, rich in tradition and meaning. It is essential to make time to reflect on our lives and find those treasures. In this collection, we have attempted to offer a sampling of family rituals and traditions for everyday living.

1

BLESSING FOR A FAMILY OR HOUSEHOLD

This rite may be used annually on a day of special significance to the family, at times when members of the family who live far apart have come together, or at times when the family experiences special difficulties or special joys. The leader may be someone from outside the family (a priest, deacon, or lay minister) or may be one of the family members. The blessing may be given at a family meal or at another appropriate time.

All make the sign of the cross. The leader begins:

Leader: The grace of our Lord Jesus Christ be with us all, now and for ever.

All: Amen.

The leader may use these words or words directed to the specific occasion to introduce the blessing;

Leader: We are a family. For one another, we are love and trial, strength and trouble. Even when far apart, we belong to one another and, in various ways, we remember and pray for one another. We join now to give thanks to our God and to ask God's blessing on this family (those who are present and those who are not here).

SCRIPTURE READING

Reader: Listen to the words of the apostle Paul to the Colossians:

Put on then, as God's chosen ones, holy and beloved, heartfelt compassion, kindness, humility, gentleness, and patience, bearing with one another and forgiving one another, if one has a grievance against another; as the Lord has forgiven you, so must you also do. And over all these put on love, that is, the bond of perfection. And let the peace of Christ control your hearts, the peace into which you were also called in one body. And be thankful. Let the word of Christ dwell in you richly, as in all wisdom you teach and admonish one another, singing psalms, hymns, and spiritual songs with gratitude in your hearts to God. And whatever you do, in word or in deed, do everything in the name of the Lord Jesus, giving thanks to God the Father through him. (Colossians 3:12–17)

(The family's Bible may be used for an alternate reading such as Ephesians 4:1–6 or 1 Corinthians 12:31–13:7.)

Reader: This is the Word of the Lord.

All: Thanks be to God.

After a time of silence, offer prayers of intercession, remembering especially those who have died. Then all join hands for the Lord's Prayer.

PRAYER OF BLESSING

(PRAYER ONE)

Leader: O God, you have created us in love and saved us in mercy, and through the bond of marriage you have established the family and willed that it should become a sign of Christ's love for his Church.

Shower your blessings on this family gathered here in your name. Enable those who are joined by one love to support one another by their fervor of spirit and devotion to prayer. Make them responsive to the need of others and witnesses to the faith in all they say and do.

We ask this through Christ our Lord.

All: Amen.

OR

(PRAYER TWO)

Leader: In good times and in bad, in sickness and in health, we belong to each other as we belong to you, God ever faithful.

By morning and by night may your name be on our lips,
a blessing to all our days:
so may kindness and patience be ever among us, a hunger
      for justice,
and songs of thankfulness in all we do.

We ask this through Christ our Lord.

All: Amen

The leader may sprinkle all with holy water, or each one may take holy water and make the sign of the cross.

Leader: May the Lord Jesus,
      who lived with his holy family in Nazareth,
      dwell also with your (our) family, keep it from all evil,
      and make all of you (us) one in heart and mind.

All: Amen.

Leader: Let us bless the Lord.

All: (Making the sign of the cross) Thanks be to God.

The blessing may conclude with singing "Now Thank We All Our God" or another appropriate song.

2

CELEBRATING GOD'S FORGIVENESS

The poet's dream of home as a place of unfailing welcome may dim from time to time, but it refuses to die. It was planted in us by the Poet who first conceived the dream, the God we call the Father. Nourish this dream in your family's heart by celebrating God's mercy and God's love. Especially on those days when peace has been restored in your household, or when you go together for sacramental reconciliation, try a simple prayer ritual like the one offered here.

BEGIN WITH PRAYER

Place a crucifix in the center of your family table or wherever you gather most comfortable for prayer. Ask family members to think about what the cross means as one person begins the prayer with these words:

God, our Father,
we needed a home,
and so you made this beautiful world.
We needed warmth and light,
and you hung the sun in the sky.

We needed food,
and you blessed the fields with rain.
We needed someone to love and care for,
and you gave us each other.
And when we quarreled and forgot your goodness,
you planted a sign of love and forgiveness
for all the world to see.
You sent your only Son to live and die for us.
He stretched out his arms on the cross
to show how you long to embrace us all.
We remember the story of Jesus,

the story of your love for us
and the love we can have for one another,
with joy and thanksgiving
today and everyday of our lives. Amen.

PRESENT A STORY

Read or retell one of the many biblical stories of forgiveness.
Or:

- Read Ezekiel 36:23–28, God's promise to warm the hard
  hearts of his people. (If you have young children—or
  children old enough to enjoy stories again—use *The
  Velveteen Rabbit*, by Margery Williams, as a parallel lesson.)

- Read John 1:1–5, 10–12, 14, 16, the poetic portion of the
  Gospel's Prologue. (*The Giving Tree*, by Shel Silverstein, is
  a modern parable of God's love.)

- Read 1 Corinthians 1:18–25, Paul's insistence that the
  cross alone reveals what God is like. (You will find a
  similar effort to create a design that will move a heart in
  Norton Justin's picture story, *The Line and the Dot*.)

Talk about the story and how it relates to your family situation.

OFFER THANKS

Offer thanks for forgiveness that graces your home by praying
together Psalm 128 or Psalm 133. Or let everyone express the
personal joy of reconciliation and offer thanks, like this:

"Tom and I found a way to resolve our differences. Thank
you, Lord."

"Mary hugged me when I told her I was sorry, and I felt
good again. Thank you, Lord."

Join hands and pray as God's family: "Our Father..."

CLOSE WITH A GESTURE

Trace the sign of the cross on one another's forehead as a reminder that you are God's children in a special way because of your baptism. Give everyone a hug and sing together "He's Got the Whole World in His Hands" (putting everyone's name into the song) or one of your family's favorites.

3

FIRST DAY/LAST DAY
OF SCHOOL

The beginning and end of each school year are important rites of passage for both the children and adults in our family. The first day of every school year is First Day Breakfast, a ritual orchestrated to marching music on the stereo. Mom or Dad cooks an elaborate breakfast, designed to fortify the kids for nine months of hard work. The most significant part of this ritual is neither the specific day nor the food served, but rather the involvement of the parent, who may not normally be home for breakfast on other mornings or be too rushed to have breakfast with the children. Adding a simple reading and prayer to the meal makes it a time of special blessing for the family.

Start your special family breakfast with one of the following readings:

> I remember you constantly in my prayers and ask the God of our Lord Jesus Christ, the glorious Father, to give you the Spirit, who will make you wise and reveal God to you, so that you will know God. I ask that your minds may be opened to see God's light, so that you will know the hope to which you have been called, the richness of the blessings God promises his people and the greatness of God's power at work in those who believe. (Ephesians, 1:17–19)

—OR—

> May grace and peace be yours from God, and in Christ Jesus the Lord...I give thanks to my God each time I remember you, and when I pray for you, I pray with joy. I cannot forget all you shared with me in the service of

the Gospel, from the first day until now. Since God began such a good work in you, I am certain that this work will be completed in the day of Christ Jesus.

This is my hope for you, for I carry you all in my heart... God knows that I love you dearly with the love of Christ Jesus, and in my prayers I ask that your love may lead you each day to a deeper knowledge and clearer discernment, that you may have good criteria for everything. So you may be pure of heart and come blameless to the day of Christ, filled with the fruit of holiness which comes through Christ Jesus, for the glory and praise of God. (Philippians 1:2–11)

Send your children off to school following the meal with this prayer:

Ever-living and ever-loving God, be with us today as we start a new school year.

Help us to learn more about ourselves, about the gifts you have given us, and how we can use them to help others grow.

Help us to learn more about the people who share this world with us. May we grow in appreciation of how special they are, and of how your love is reflected through them.

Help us to learn more about the world in which we live. May we see our connectedness with all of creation and learn what we can do to build a world where the world's goodness is shared by all.

We ask this with confidence in the name of Jesus. Amen.

The last day of school can be a time to celebrate new learnings, new friendships and all the accomplishments of the year...and to welcome in summer as a time of recreation. Mark the end of the school year with a special supper meal. Incorporate the following components.

SCRIPTURE: Matthew 4:14-16 or Psalm 36: 5-10

LITANY OF THANKSGIVING: Invite family members to recognize the ways they have grown in relationships and knowledge through the year. Invite them to mention the specific people and events for which they are thankful, and the opportunities for growth which the year provided. Respond simply to each item with the phrase: We thank you!

PRAYER OF BLESSING: Close your sharing with the following blessing:

We give you thanks, loving God, for the gifts we have been given. May we continue to share these gifts with one another and with the world around us. Keep us open to the new possibilities for growth and recreation that the summer provides. May we see in all creation a reminder of your constant love for us. Amen.

OPTION: A small gift for each child, marking the efforts and accomplishments of the year, can be presented over a special dessert.

4

MEAL TIMES

BLESSINGS BEFORE MEALS

I.
Lord God and Giver of All Good Gifts,
we are grateful as we pause before this meal,
for all the blessings of life that you give to us.

Daily, we are fed with good things,
nourished by friendship and care,
feasted with forgiveness and understanding.

And so, mindful of your continuous care,
we pause to be grateful for the blessings of this table.
(Pause for silent reflection)

May your presence be the "extra" taste to this meal
which we eat in the name of your Son, Jesus.
Amen✠

II.
The day is coming to a close,
and, like the disciples on the road to Emmaus,
we pause to break bread together.

May our eyes be opened,
and, in this act of common sharing,
may we see the risen Lord in one another.

May we see the Lord of Life in our food,
our conversation and lives shared in common.
May these gifts strengthen us to continue your work in our
world.

May the blessing of God, his peace and love,
rest upon our table.
Amen✠

THANKSGIVING AFTER MEALS

I.
We thank you, our God,
for the food you have given us.
May our sharing this bread together
lead to a renewal of our communion with you,
with one another, and with all creatures.

We ask this through Christ our Lord.
Amen✠

II.
Lord, you feed every living thing.
We have eaten together at this table;
keep us in your love.

Give us true concern for the least of our sisters and brothers,
so that as we gladly share our food with them,
we may also sit down together with them
at the table of the kingdom of heaven.

We ask this through Christ our Lord.
Amen✠

III.
Lord, you have fed us from your gifts and favors;
fill us with your mercy,
for you live and reign for ever and ever.
Amen✠

STEPFAMILY SUPPER

Given that life is very hectic and involved, and also that
members of many stepfamilies find themselves spending time
and eating in a number of households in any given week, one
stepfamily found it important to establish one particular late
afternoon (post-school hours) and dinner time per week to be
together. Eating and talking together like this, at least once a
week, provided the chance to tell a number of stories, resolve

family issues, plan upcoming stepfamily events and vacations, share some humor, and recognize God's ongoing presence in our lives. Here are several important guidelines:

1. All television and media sources should be turned off.
2. Set the table completely. Try using a table cloth and candles for an extra touch.
3. Serve a complete dinner from soup to dessert.
4. Begin dinner by holding hands and praying. Each week someone is assigned to lead prayer on a rotation basis.
5. Allow at least an hour for eating and conversation. Don't be afraid to linger over dessert and coffee.
6. Make sure everyone has an opportunity to share about one significant event from the past week.
7. Everyone takes part in cleaning up, too!

SHARING MEALS

Although our lives are hectic, we have made a conscious effort to reinforce the importance of having one meal together. Everyone participates, in some capacity, in the preparation of the meal. Some days the children help to plan the meal or help to prepare it. Other days they set the table (which might include some seasonal decoration) or choose some appropriate music for dinner.

We begin our meal by praying the traditional grace before meals and include special prayers, e.g., for a friend who is sick, thanks for beautiful weather, or acknowledging a special time for our family. We discuss the daily occurrences in our lives, news events, politics, and reflect on Sunday Scriptures. My spouse and I believe this is a teachable moment in our lives. During the meal, we always eat at the table, the television and radio are off and we do not talk on the telephone—this is family time.

Those who did not help in the preparation of the meal are responsible for the clean up. This time has become so important to our children that they choose not to participate in activities which are scheduled during the dinner hour and strongly encourage us to do the same.

MEAL-TIME PRAYER

Although my parents were not both Catholic, we always said the traditional "Grace before Meals" before dinner. It became such an accepted ritual that none of us felt comfortable eating a bite before "prayers." In fact, we even developed a special "family pause" in the middle (to allow little ones to catch their breath). When my own children were small, the tradition continued. That quiet moment of prayer allows us to focus on our time together at table, even when demanding schedules may not allow an otherwise leisurely meal.

Over the years, I have watched with interest the effect of our prayer on young guests at our table. One young adolescent, after several meals with us, actually asked to learn the prayer so she could say it too. Others, after a moment of awkwardness, seem to actually like the opportunity to share a "quiet moment." My own children, now adolescents, have never seemed reluctant or self-conscious about this family ritual. In fact, when meal-time is particularly rushed or unorganized, they are the ones who will remind us all with the question, "Did we pray?"

MEAL-TIME LITANY

At mealtime, at the end of the blessing, our family would always say, "God bless Mom and Dad and Pat" and individually name each person in the family. It eventually developed into a blessing for others—for anyone whom a family member wanted to remember, such as a friend at school who was having a hard time, or maybe someone who had a death in the family. Now we have grandchildren. When they come to the house, they like to include their little friends from kindergarten. It has been very rewarding. Our married children are continuing this ritual in their families.

BLESSINGS FOR COMING AND GOING

GOODBYE BLESSING

When children are preparing to leave home, they often have ambivalent feelings. While they are eager to start their own lives, they may be frightened as well and embarrassed to admit their anxieties.

Why not give a child who is going out something special to hold on to? One idea that comes to mind is a geode, those rocks that started off undistinguished but under the press of time and weight became full of glittering facets.

Another suggestion might be a family moment in which the person who is leaving is blessed by the parents: "May the Lord bless you and keep you in your coming in and your going out. May the face of the Lord shine upon you and be gracious unto you." Those, or other personal words might be spoken at a family going-away dinner or at a breakfast before each departure. Words do not give us strength, but the power of caring and commitment that words can convey do make us feel stronger and braver.

SUNRISE SERVICE

When awakening my children each morning, I take a few minutes to observe them in their slumber. Watching them sleep I lift a silent prayer of thanksgiving for their presence in my life and ask for God's guidance over them during the day. Then I gently rub their backs and wake them up. This provides a peaceful transition to the day and also allows for some physical contact which we all need.

MORNING DEPARTURE

Each day before we depart to our various destination we say good-bye and hug one another. As the children have gotten older, they are not comfortable doing this in front of their friends so we make a point of saying good-bye in our home. Incorporate a simple blessing, like:

May God be with you in everything you do today.

May your day be blessed with new life, new learnings, and the company of friends.

BEDTIME BLESSINGS

In our household, we have a simple ritual that has become a never omitted part of the bedtime routine. It began when Katie was an infant. When we put her down for the night, we would trace a cross on her forehead, followed by a kiss. The first few times I remember feeling awkward, yet it felt peaceful to ask God's blessing on her while she slept. As she grew into toddlerhood, the bedtime routine expanded to include a book, a song, her simple prayer, and the blessing by both her Dad and me. The preschooler added a chat about her day, and there were times when she would summon us to her room with the question, "Did you bless me?" before she would drift off to sleep. Even when there were overnight guests, the visiting children would look expectantly at me to trace a cross on their foreheads. The advent of third grade has brought a new development. Katie now blesses both her Dad and me before she falls asleep. The ritual seems to have become so much a part of her that she chooses to reciprocate. Perhaps it's her maturation or her awareness of a religious practice that she can initiate. Whatever the reason, pajamas, a story, a chat, a song, prayer, and blessing provide a relaxing, comforting joy-filled close to our day. A larger family might group portions of this kind of daily routine, but a few moments spent with each child individually signing them and sealing it with a kiss offers a very holy moment in the midst of the messiness of family life.

QUIET TIME

As our children were growing up, my husband and I always took time when he came home from work to have some "quiet time" together. It was a time, usually a half hour, when he and I could catch up on one another's life, share the hopes and concerns that grew from our day's experience, and ask for God's continued guidance and presence in our lives. We would make arrangements for the children to have some activity to keep them busy so we could have this important time together. This brief time of prayer and sharing helped set a tone for our evening together as a family, and strengthened our relationship as husband and wife.